50 Greatest Moments in Sports

Dr. Robert H. Stauffer Jr.

Published by Robert Stauffer, 2024.

50 GREATEST MOMENTS IN SPORTS

First edition. September 3, 2024.

Copyright © 2024 Dr. Robert H. Stauffer Jr..

ISBN: 979-8224300921

Written by Dr. Robert H. Stauffer Jr..

Table of Contents

50 Greatest Moments in Sports History: An Unforgettable Journey Through Athletic Excellence

The purpose of the book is to delve into the most iconic moments in sports history, shedding light on their profound significance, the impact they had on the world, and the powerful emotions they stirred in fans and athletes alike. By chronicling these unforgettable events, the book aims to not only celebrate athletic achievements but also to explore how these moments transcended the boundaries of sports, influencing culture, society, and inspiring generations across the globe. Through detailed narratives and thoughtful analysis, the book will offer readers a deeper understanding of why these moments are etched in the collective memory and how they continue to resonate today.

The importance of sports moments lies in their ability to transcend the boundaries of the games themselves, becoming much more than just victories or records. These moments often reflect and shape the culture of their time, serving as catalysts for change, symbols of perseverance, and sources of inspiration for people across the globe.

When Jesse Owens triumphed at the 1936 Berlin Olympics, it wasn't just a win on the track; it was a powerful statement against the ideology of racial superiority, challenging societal norms and inspiring the civil rights movement. Similarly, Jackie Robinson breaking Major League Baseball's color barrier in 1947 wasn't just about playing a game; it marked a pivotal moment in the fight for racial equality in America.

Sports moments also inspire generations by demonstrating the heights of human potential, resilience, and determination. Muhammad Ali's victory over George Foreman in the "Rumble in the Jungle" was not just a boxing match, but a testament to the power of self-belief and the fight against adversity. These moments provide people with heroes to look up to, stories to draw strength from, and dreams to aspire to, far beyond the realm of sports.

Moreover, many iconic sports moments reflect broader societal changes, acting as mirrors of their times. Billie Jean King's victory over Bobby Riggs in the 1973 "Battle of the Sexes" symbolized the growing movement for gender equality, while the Miracle on Ice in 1980 resonated as a Cold War triumph, reflecting national pride and resilience. These moments resonate because they are more than just sports; they are integral parts of our collective history, shaping and reflecting the world around them.

The structure of the book will be organized thematically, allowing readers to explore the greatest moments in sports history through a variety of lenses. This approach will help to connect moments across different sports and eras, revealing the underlying themes that make these events so impactful. Each chapter will focus on a specific theme, weaving together stories from different sports and time periods that share common threads.

Thematic Organization:

1. Early Legends and Pioneers: This chapter will highlight the foundational moments in sports history, featuring early legends who broke barriers and set the stage for future generations. It will cover pioneering achievements that defined the early 20th century, showcasing the rise of sports as a global phenomenon.
2. Defying the Odds: Focused on moments where athletes and teams overcame incredible obstacles, this chapter will explore underdog victories, comebacks, and feats of perseverance that captured the world's imagination.
3. Olympic Glory: Dedicated to the most iconic moments in Olympic history, this chapter will span decades of athletic achievement on the world's biggest stage, celebrating the

unity, competition, and personal triumphs that define the Olympics.

4. Basketball's Finest Moments: A chapter devoted to the defining moments in basketball history, from record-breaking performances to unforgettable games, highlighting how the sport has evolved and impacted culture globally.

5. Football Feats: This chapter will capture the greatest moments in American football, showcasing legendary plays, Super Bowl triumphs, and the athletes who redefined the game.

6. Iconic World Cup Moments: Covering soccer's most significant global stage, this chapter will explore moments from the World Cup that not only defined the sport but also reflected broader social and political themes.

7. Unstoppable Forces in Tennis: Featuring the greatest achievements in tennis, this chapter will focus on record-setting performances and landmark victories that have shaped the sport's history.

8. Triumphs in the Face of Adversity: This chapter will delve into stories of athletes who faced personal, physical, or societal challenges and still managed to achieve greatness, inspiring millions.

9. Legendary Moments in Baseball: Highlighting baseball's most memorable moments, this chapter will explore feats that have become legendary in American culture, from the World Series to individual achievements.

10. Modern Marvels: A chapter focusing on the more recent sports history, featuring moments from the 21st century that continue to shape the narrative of sports today.

11. Shocking Upsets and Unlikely Victories: This chapter will cover the moments that defied expectations, where underdogs triumphed against all odds, shocking the world

and leaving an indelible mark on sports history.

12. Motorsport Milestones: Highlighting key moments in motorsport history, this chapter will celebrate the speed, precision, and innovation that define the world of racing.

13. Unforgettable Team Triumphs: Focusing on team sports, this chapter will recount moments where collaboration, strategy, and unity led to unforgettable victories and championship titles.

14. Moments That Redefined Sports: This chapter will explore the moments that changed the way we see and understand sports, whether through innovation, social impact, or cultural significance.

15. Iconic Moments of Skill and Precision: A chapter dedicated to showcasing moments of unparalleled skill, precision, and mastery across various sports, celebrating the art of athletic excellence.

16. The Next Generation of Greatness: Concluding the book, this chapter will highlight recent and emerging moments that signal the future of sports, featuring young athletes and evolving trends that continue to captivate and inspire.

Chapter 1: Early Legends and Pioneers

Jesse Owens at the 1936 Berlin Olympics

Context of the Berlin Olympics and Nazi Germany:

The 1936 Berlin Olympics were more than just a global sporting event; they were a stage for Adolf Hitler's Nazi regime to showcase its ideology of Aryan supremacy. Hitler saw the Olympics as an opportunity to demonstrate the supposed superiority of the Aryan race to the world. The games were meticulously orchestrated to reflect the strength, order, and dominance of Nazi Germany, with the international community watching closely. However, the presence of African American athletes, particularly Jesse Owens, posed a direct challenge to the Nazi racial doctrine.

Owens' Four Gold Medals and Their Impact on Civil Rights and International Relations:

Jesse Owens, an African American track and field athlete, emerged as the star of the 1936 Olympics, winning four gold medals in the 100 meters, 200 meters, long jump, and 4x100 meter relay. His remarkable achievements not only shattered the Nazi myth of racial superiority but also became a powerful symbol of resistance against oppression and racism.

Owens' victories on German soil had a profound impact on the civil rights movement in the United States. At a time when segregation and racial discrimination were rampant, Owens' success provided hope and inspiration to African Americans. He became a symbol of excellence and defiance against the racist ideologies that sought to marginalize him both in Germany and in his own country.

Internationally, Owens' triumphs challenged the legitimacy of Hitler's propaganda and exposed the hypocrisy of the Nazi regime. His performances garnered global attention, leading to widespread admiration and respect, even from those within Germany who were disillusioned with Nazi ideology. Owens' victories also strained the relationship between the United States and Nazi Germany, as his success contradicted the very foundation of the Nazi racial doctrine.

Despite his historic achievements, Owens returned to a segregated America where he continued to face racial discrimination. However, his legacy endured, and his victories at the Berlin Olympics became a catalyst for future progress in the fight for civil rights. Owens' story remains a powerful reminder of how sports can transcend political and social boundaries, challenging ideologies and inspiring change on a global scale.

In sum, Jesse Owens' performance at the 1936 Berlin Olympics was not just a remarkable athletic achievement but a moment that reverberated far beyond the track, influencing civil rights and international relations for decades to come. His story is a testament to the power of sports to challenge injustice and bring about societal change.

Babe Ruth's Called Shot (1932)

The Legendary Home Run in the World Series:

On October 1, 1932, during Game 3 of the World Series between the New York Yankees and the Chicago Cubs, one of the most iconic moments in baseball history unfolded—Babe Ruth's "Called Shot." Playing at Wrigley Field, the game was intense, with the Cubs' players and fans heckling Ruth throughout. In the fifth inning, with the score tied 4-4, Ruth came to bat. After taking two strikes, Ruth made a gesture—either pointing to center field or towards the pitcher, depending on the account—which many interpreted as him predicting or "calling" his next hit.

On the very next pitch, Ruth swung and sent the ball soaring deep into the center field stands for a home run. The crowd was stunned, and the legend of the "Called Shot" was born. This home run helped propel the Yankees to a 7-5 victory in that game and a subsequent sweep of the Cubs in the series. While the exact details of whether Ruth truly called his shot remain a subject of debate, the moment has become a part of baseball folklore, symbolizing Ruth's confidence, charisma, and larger-than-life persona.

Lasting Legacy:

The "Called Shot" has transcended the sport, becoming one of the most legendary moments in baseball and American sports history. Babe Ruth's gesture, whether intentional or not, epitomizes the mystique and bravado that defined his career and made him a cultural icon. The story of the Called Shot has been passed down through generations, embodying the spirit of baseball—a game where myth and reality often blend.

Ruth's Called Shot also contributed to his enduring legacy as one of the greatest and most charismatic athletes in history. It encapsulates the excitement and unpredictability of sports, where a single moment can become immortal. The legend of the Called Shot continues to inspire and entertain, serving as a reminder of the power of sports to create unforgettable moments that live on long after the game is over.

Moreover, the Called Shot has been referenced and celebrated in popular culture, reinforcing its status as a symbol of confidence and greatness. It has been depicted in films, documentaries, and even cartoons, further embedding the moment in the collective consciousness of sports fans around the world.

In summary, Babe Ruth's Called Shot during the 1932 World Series is more than just a home run; it is a defining moment in sports history, representing the audacity and flair that made Ruth a legend. Its lasting legacy continues to captivate baseball fans and remains an iconic example of how sports moments can transcend the game and become a part of cultural history.

Roger Bannister Breaks the 4-Minute Mile (1954)

The Significance of Breaking a Seemingly Impossible Barrier:

On May 6, 1954, Roger Bannister, a 25-year-old British medical student, achieved what many thought was impossible—he became the first person to run a mile in under four minutes. Bannister's time of 3 minutes and 59.4 seconds, set at Oxford University's Iffley Road track, shattered a psychological and physical barrier that had stood for decades.

Before Bannister's accomplishment, the four-minute mile was widely regarded as an insurmountable limit for human endurance. Medical experts, coaches, and athletes believed that the human body was simply not capable of sustaining the speed required to break the four-minute mark. The quest to break this barrier had become one of the greatest challenges in athletics, with numerous athletes attempting and failing to achieve the feat.

Bannister's success was the culmination of meticulous planning, intense training, and a scientific approach to running. He carefully calculated his pace, focused on optimal running conditions, and was aided by pacemakers Chris Brasher and Chris Chataway, who set the tempo for the first three laps. As Bannister sprinted down the final stretch, the crowd's excitement grew, and when the announcer declared his time, the world knew that history had been made.

The significance of Bannister breaking the four-minute mile extends far beyond the world of athletics. It represented a triumph of the human spirit and the power of belief. Bannister's achievement showed that perceived limitations could be overcome with determination, innovation, and perseverance. His success inspired not only runners but also people in all walks of life to push beyond their own boundaries and strive for what was once thought impossible.

Bannister's record-breaking run also had a profound impact on the sport of middle-distance running. In the years following his achievement, numerous athletes broke the four-minute barrier, demonstrating that once the psychological barrier was removed, others could achieve it as well. Bannister's feat marked the beginning of a new era in athletics, where breaking records became a matter of pushing the limits rather than accepting them.

In a broader sense, Bannister's accomplishment symbolized the post-war era's optimism and the belief in progress and human potential. His run came at a time when the world was rebuilding and looking for new heroes, and Bannister's triumph provided inspiration on a global scale.

In summary, Roger Bannister's breaking of the four-minute mile in 1954 was a landmark moment in sports history. It was not just a physical achievement, but a symbolic victory over perceived limits, inspiring countless others to challenge what is possible. Bannister's run remains a powerful reminder of the resilience and potential of the human spirit, making it one of the greatest moments in sports history.

Chapter 2: Defying the Odds

Jackie Robinson Breaks the Color Barrier (1947)

The Challenges and Triumphs of Integrating Major League Baseball:

On April 15, 1947, Jackie Robinson made history by stepping onto Ebbets Field in Brooklyn, New York, as the first African American player in Major League Baseball (MLB) in the modern era. His debut for the Brooklyn Dodgers was a watershed moment, not just for baseball, but for American society as a whole. Robinson's integration into MLB broke the color barrier that had segregated the sport for more than 50 years, paving the way for future generations of athletes and contributing to the broader Civil Rights Movement.

Challenges:

Robinson faced immense challenges both on and off the field. Despite his exceptional talent, he was met with hostility, racism, and discrimination from fans, opposing players, and even some of his teammates. He endured racial slurs, threats of violence, and attempts to intimidate him, all while being scrutinized by the press and the public. Robinson was under immense pressure to perform at the highest level while maintaining his composure, as any outburst or failure could have been used as justification to reinforce the racist beliefs of those who opposed integration.

The burden placed on Robinson was not just physical but also psychological. He had to adhere to a promise made to Dodgers' general manager Branch Rickey, who had signed Robinson to the team, that he would not retaliate against the inevitable provocation. This "noble experiment," as Rickey called it, required Robinson to exhibit extraordinary courage, patience, and resilience. His ability to withstand this pressure while excelling on the field was a testament to his strength of character and commitment to the cause of integration.

Triumphs:

Despite the overwhelming challenges, Robinson's impact on the field was immediate and profound. He won the Rookie of the Year Award in 1947, leading the National League in stolen bases and helping the Dodgers win the pennant. His success not only silenced many critics but also demonstrated that talent and determination know no racial boundaries. Over the course of his career, Robinson was named to six All-Star teams, won the National League MVP in 1949, and led the Dodgers to six World Series appearances, including a championship in 1955.

Robinson's integration into Major League Baseball had far-reaching implications beyond the sport. It was a significant step forward in the struggle for civil rights in America. His presence on the field challenged the segregationist norms of the time and inspired other sectors of society to reconsider their own practices of exclusion. Robinson's success showed that breaking down racial barriers was not only possible but beneficial, helping to accelerate the push for equality across the nation.

Jackie Robinson's legacy extends far beyond his statistics and accomplishments in baseball. He became a symbol of progress, courage, and the fight for justice. His pioneering role in integrating MLB paved the way for countless African American athletes who followed in his footsteps and contributed to the eventual desegregation of other areas of American life. His number, 42, has since been retired across all of Major League Baseball, a rare honor that underscores the significance of his contribution to the sport and society.

In summary, Jackie Robinson's breaking of the color barrier in 1947 was a monumental achievement that transcended baseball. It was a triumph of determination, resilience, and the pursuit of equality in the face of systemic racism. Robinson's courage in the face of adversity not only changed the sport forever but also played a crucial role in the broader struggle for civil rights in the United States, making it one of the greatest moments in sports history.

Jackie Robinson's breaking of the color barrier in Major League Baseball (MLB) had a profound and lasting impact on the Civil Rights Movement in the United States. His success on the baseball field became a powerful symbol of the broader struggle for racial equality and justice, influencing both the social and political landscapes of the time.

Catalyst for Social Change: Robinson's integration into MLB in 1947 challenged the deeply entrenched system of segregation that defined American society. At a time when racial discrimination was legally enforced in many parts of the country, Robinson's presence on the field as the first African American player in modern MLB was a direct challenge to the status quo. His ability to succeed in a white-dominated sport under such intense scrutiny and hostility served as a powerful demonstration that African Americans could compete and excel on equal footing with whites.

Inspiration for the Civil Rights Movement:

Robinson's courage and perseverance became a source of inspiration for the burgeoning Civil Rights Movement. His achievements on the field provided a visible, tangible example of the fight against racial injustice, giving hope and motivation to African Americans and civil rights activists. Robinson's success showed that breaking down racial barriers was not only possible but necessary, reinforcing the ideals of equality and justice that would drive the movement in the coming years.

Prominent civil rights leaders, including Martin Luther King Jr., often cited Robinson as a trailblazer whose actions paved the way for the broader push for desegregation. King once remarked that Robinson "was a sit-inner before sit-ins, a freedom rider before freedom rides," underscoring Robinson's role as a forerunner of the direct action that characterized the Civil Rights Movement in the 1950s and 1960s.

Economic and Social Impact:

Robinson's success also had an economic and social impact, particularly within the African American community. As Robinson became a star player, African Americans felt a sense of pride and ownership in his achievements, which helped to elevate the status and visibility of black athletes in other sports as well. This increased visibility contributed to a gradual change in public attitudes towards African Americans, helping to erode some of the prejudices that had justified segregation.

Moreover, Robinson's integration into MLB helped to open doors for other African American players, who soon followed in his footsteps. As more black athletes entered professional sports, the visibility of African Americans in mainstream American life increased, challenging stereotypes and fostering greater acceptance and integration in other areas of society.

Political Impact:

Robinson's influence extended into the political arena as well. He used his platform to speak out against racism and injustice, becoming an advocate for civil rights both during and after his baseball career. He was outspoken in his support for desegregation and worked with civil rights organizations to promote equality. Robinson's activism demonstrated the potential for athletes to influence political and social issues, a legacy that continues to this day.

Robinson's breaking of the color barrier also had implications for U.S. relations with the rest of the world. At the height of the Cold War, the United States was keenly aware of how its racial policies were perceived internationally. Robinson's integration into MLB was seen as a positive step in addressing the racial inequalities that were often criticized by America's adversaries, helping to improve the nation's image abroad.

Legacy:

The impact of Jackie Robinson's breakthrough on civil rights is still felt today. His courage and determination helped to lay the groundwork for the Civil Rights Movement, and his legacy continues to inspire athletes and activists alike. Robinson's story is a reminder of the power of sports to drive social change and challenge injustice, making his achievements not just a pivotal moment in sports history, but a significant chapter in the ongoing struggle for civil rights in America.

In summary, Jackie Robinson's integration into Major League Baseball was a catalyst for the Civil Rights Movement, providing a powerful symbol of progress and equality. His success challenged the foundations of segregation, inspired activists, and helped to change the social and political landscape of the United States, making his impact on civil rights profound and enduring.

Secretariat's Belmont Stakes Win (1973)

The Achievement:

Secretariat's victory in the 1973 Belmont Stakes is widely regarded as one of the most dominant performances in horse racing history. His win not only secured the Triple Crown but also set a world record that stands to this day, solidifying his legacy as one of the greatest racehorses of all time.

Context and Background:

1. Secretariat's Background:

o Early Career: Secretariat, a chestnut colt trained by Lucien Laurin and owned by Penny Chenery of Meadow Stable, was born on March 30, 1970. He quickly established himself as a talented and competitive racehorse with impressive performances early in his career.

o Triple Crown Bid: By 1973, Secretariat had already won the Kentucky Derby and the Preakness Stakes, positioning him to potentially achieve the Triple Crown—a feat accomplished by only a few horses in history.

2. The 1973 Belmont Stakes:

o Race Context: The Belmont Stakes, held on June 9, 1973, at Belmont Park in Elmont, New York, was the final leg of the Triple Crown. Secretariat entered the race as the favorite, with high expectations following his victories in the earlier Triple Crown races.

o Field and Competition: The field for the Belmont Stakes included several competitors, but Secretariat's reputation and prior performances made him the standout horse.

The Race:
1. Performance:

o Dominant Display: Secretariat's performance in the Belmont Stakes was nothing short of extraordinary. He led the race from start to finish, pulling away from the competition with a remarkable display of speed and stamina.

o Record Setting: Secretariat crossed the finish line with a time of 2:24, setting a world record for the 1½-mile distance. His margin of victory was an astonishing 31 lengths, an unprecedented and unmatched achievement in the history of horse racing.

2. The Crowd and Atmosphere:

o Spectator Reactions: The crowd at Belmont Park was awestruck by Secretariat's performance. The race was met with widespread acclaim and admiration, as fans and experts alike marveled at the horse's sheer dominance.

o Historical Significance: Secretariat's victory was celebrated as a historic moment in horse racing, and his performance was widely regarded as one of the greatest in the sport's history.

Impact and Significance:
1. Legacy of Dominance:

o Triple Crown Achievement: Secretariat's win in the Belmont Stakes completed his Triple Crown, cementing his place as one of the most legendary horses in racing history. His dominance in all three races was a testament to his exceptional ability and versatility.

o Record Streak: The world record set by Secretariat in the Belmont Stakes remains unbeaten, underscoring the extraordinary nature of his performance and the difficulty of achieving such a feat.

2. Cultural and Popular Impact:

o National Fame: Secretariat's achievements brought him national fame and endeared him to a broad audience. His story captured the imagination of sports fans and horse racing enthusiasts, becoming a symbol of excellence and greatness.

o Media and Popular Culture: Secretariat's Belmont Stakes performance was widely covered in the media and has been celebrated in various forms of popular culture, including books, documentaries, and films. His legacy continues to be a source of inspiration and fascination.

3. Influence on Horse Racing:

o Benchmark for Greatness: Secretariat's performance set a new benchmark for greatness in horse racing. His achievements are frequently referenced in discussions about the greatest racehorses of all time, and his name is synonymous with dominance and excellence in the sport.

o Impact on Future Generations: Secretariat's legacy has influenced and inspired subsequent generations of racehorses, trainers, and fans. His story serves as a reminder of the possibilities of greatness in horse racing and the impact of extraordinary talent and performance.

Conclusion:
Secretariat's Belmont Stakes win in 1973 is an iconic moment in sports history, representing the pinnacle of dominance in horse racing. His record-setting performance and Triple Crown victory solidified his status as one of the greatest racehorses of all time. The race remains a defining moment in the sport, celebrated for its extraordinary display of speed, stamina, and excellence. Secretariat's legacy endures as a symbol of greatness and continues to inspire admiration and respect within the horse racing community and beyond.

Muhammad Ali's "Fight of the Century" vs. Joe Frazier

(1971)

The Cultural and Political Significance of Ali's Fight and Legacy:

On March 8, 1971, Madison Square Garden in New York City played host to one of boxing's most anticipated and historic bouts—the "Fight of the Century" between Muhammad Ali and Joe Frazier. This match, which saw Frazier defeat Ali by unanimous decision, was more than just a clash between two elite fighters; it was a cultural and political event that reflected the turbulent social and political climate of the early 1970s.

Cultural Significance:

1. The Boxing Spectacle: The fight was dubbed the "Fight of the Century" due to the high stakes involved. It was the first time in history that two undefeated heavyweight champions faced each other in the ring. Both Ali and Frazier were at the peak of their powers, and their clash was eagerly anticipated by boxing fans and the general public alike. The match was a global spectacle, attracting attention from around the world and drawing a record-breaking crowd to Madison Square Garden.

2. Ali's Charismatic Persona: Muhammad Ali, known for his charisma, brashness, and poetic trash talk, was a larger-than-life figure whose presence transcended the sport of boxing. His outspoken personality, combined with his exceptional boxing skills, made him a cultural icon. Ali's fight with Frazier was not just about boxing prowess but also about Ali's larger-than-life persona and the public's fascination with his career and life.

Political Significance:

1. Ali's Political and Social Stance: Muhammad Ali was not just a sports figure; he was also a prominent political and social activist. His refusal to be drafted into the Vietnam War, citing his religious beliefs and opposition to the war, led to his suspension from boxing and the stripping of his titles. Ali's stance made him a polarizing figure, celebrated by some as a courageous champion of civil rights and criticized by others who saw him as unpatriotic. The "Fight of the Century" was therefore not only a boxing match but also a symbol of Ali's complex relationship with American society and politics.

2. Integration of Politics and Sports: The fight between Ali and Frazier occurred during a period of significant social upheaval in the United States. The 1960s and early 1970s were marked by civil rights struggles, anti-war protests, and a growing questioning of authority. Ali's defiance of the draft and his role in the Civil Rights Movement made him a symbol of resistance and defiance against the establishment. The fight with Frazier was viewed through the lens of these broader societal conflicts, adding layers of political and cultural significance to the event.

Legacy:

1. Impact on Boxing and Sports: The "Fight of the Century" remains one of the most famous bouts in boxing history. The match showcased the extraordinary talents of both fighters and highlighted the dramatic intensity that boxing can offer. It also set a high standard for future high-profile boxing matches and is often cited as a key moment in the sport's history.

2. Ali's Enduring Influence: Muhammad Ali's legacy extends far beyond his achievements in the ring. He became a global ambassador for peace and humanitarian causes, and his

impact on sports and society has been profound. The "Fight of the Century" is a pivotal moment in Ali's career, representing both his triumphs and challenges. Ali's ability to rise above adversity and his contributions to social change continue to be celebrated and remembered.

3. Cultural Reflection: The fight and its aftermath reflect the broader cultural and political shifts of the era. Ali's public persona, his legal battles, and his political activism were central to the discourse of the time. The fight with Frazier symbolized the intersection of sports and politics, illustrating how major sporting events can serve as a stage for broader societal issues.

Conclusion:

Muhammad Ali's "Fight of the Century" against Joe Frazier in 1971 was a landmark event with significant cultural and political implications. The bout was not only a showcase of boxing excellence but also a reflection of the era's social and political tensions. The fight's legacy endures as a testament to Ali's impact on both sports and society, highlighting the ways in which athletic achievements can intersect with and influence broader cultural and political movements.

Muhammad Ali's activism extended far beyond the boxing ring and made a profound impact on both American society and the global stage. His activism was marked by his strong stance on various social, political, and humanitarian issues. Here are some key aspects of Ali's activism:

1. Opposition to the Vietnam War:

• Draft Refusal: Muhammad Ali's refusal to be drafted into the Vietnam War was one of the most significant acts of his activism. In 1966, he declared that he was conscientiously opposed to the war on religious and moral grounds. Ali, a member of the Nation of Islam, argued that the war was unjust and that his religious beliefs prohibited him from participating. His famous statement, "I ain't got no quarrel with them Viet Cong," captured his stance and resonated with many who opposed the war.

• Legal and Personal Consequences: Ali's stance led to significant repercussions. He was stripped of his boxing titles, banned from the sport, and faced a five-year prison sentence. His case was eventually taken up by the Supreme Court, which overturned his conviction in 1971, but during this period, he was effectively barred from competing, which significantly impacted his career.

2. Civil Rights and Racial Equality:

• Champion of Civil Rights: Ali was a vocal advocate for civil rights and racial equality. His association with the Nation of Islam and his conversion to Islam highlighted his commitment to challenging racial injustice and advocating for African American empowerment. Ali's public persona and outspoken views brought attention to issues of racial inequality and civil rights, making him a symbol of the struggle for racial justice.

• Support for Black Power Movement: Ali's alignment with the Black Power movement and his relationships with figures such as Malcolm X and the leaders of the Nation of Islam underscored his commitment to advancing the cause of African American rights. His activism contributed to raising awareness about racial issues and inspired others in the fight for equality.

3. Advocacy for Humanitarian Causes:

• Global Humanitarian Efforts: Beyond his domestic activism, Ali engaged in numerous humanitarian efforts around the world. He traveled extensively to promote peace and aid, using his fame to support various causes. Notably, Ali was involved in humanitarian missions in countries like Nigeria and Uganda, where he worked to alleviate suffering and promote diplomacy.

• Support for Refugees and the Poor: Ali used his platform to advocate for the rights of refugees and the poor. His efforts included fundraising and raising awareness for organizations that provided aid to those in need. His humanitarian work often intersected with his advocacy for peace and justice, demonstrating his commitment to improving the lives of the disadvantaged.

4. Advocacy Against Racial and Social Injustice:

• Combatting Racism and Injustice: Throughout his career, Ali was outspoken against racism and social injustice. He used his position to challenge systemic inequalities and confront prejudice, both within and outside the realm of sports. His public statements and actions were aimed at confronting and dismantling discriminatory practices and fostering greater understanding.

• Influence on Future Activists: Ali's activism served as a powerful example for future generations of athletes and activists. His willingness to use his platform for social change inspired many to follow in his footsteps and address issues of social justice and human rights. Ali's legacy as an activist continues to influence contemporary discussions on race, justice, and equality.

5. Post-Retirement Advocacy:

• Fight Against Parkinson's Disease: After retiring from boxing, Ali was diagnosed with Parkinson's disease, a condition he would battle for the rest of his life. He became an advocate for research into Parkinson's and other neurological diseases, using his own experience to raise awareness and support for medical research.

• Peace and Diplomacy: In his later years, Ali continued to be involved in efforts to promote peace and resolve conflicts. His efforts included meeting with world leaders and participating in diplomatic missions to foster understanding and cooperation between nations.

Conclusion:

Muhammad Ali's activism was integral to his legacy, showcasing his commitment to social justice, racial equality, and humanitarian causes. His courage to stand up against the Vietnam War draft, his advocacy for civil rights, and his global humanitarian efforts all contributed to his status as not just a sports icon, but a prominent and influential figure in the broader struggle for social change. Ali's activism continues to inspire and resonate, reflecting his profound impact on both his era and the world beyond boxing.

Chapter 3: Olympic Glory

<u>Nadia Comăneci's Perfect 10 (1976)</u>

The Historic Achievement:

On July 18, 1976, at the Montreal Summer Olympics, 14-year-old Nadia Comăneci of Romania made history by scoring the first perfect 10 in Olympic gymnastics. Her flawless performance on the uneven bars during the gymnastics competition captivated the world and marked a milestone in the sport's history.

Details of the Performance:

● Routine on the Uneven Bars: Comăneci's routine on the uneven bars was executed with unprecedented precision and artistry. Her performance was characterized by perfect execution of moves, exceptional technique, and flawless execution of transitions. The judges, initially unsure of how to score a perfect routine, eventually awarded her a perfect 10, a score that had never been given before in Olympic gymnastics.

● Immediate Reaction: The announcement of Comăneci's perfect score was met with astonishment from the audience and the gymnastics community. The scoreboard was not equipped to display a score of 10, so it initially showed a score of 1.00 before being updated to reflect the historic achievement.

Impact on Gymnastics:

1. Raising the Bar for Gymnastics: Comăneci's perfect 10 set a new standard for gymnastics performance. Her flawless routine demonstrated that a perfect score was achievable, leading to a higher level of competition and inspiring gymnasts around the world to push the boundaries of the sport. The achievement redefined the expectations for precision and execution in gymnastics.

2. Inspiration for Future Gymnasts: Nadia Comăneci became an icon and a role model for future generations of gymnasts. Her success highlighted the possibilities within the sport, inspiring young athletes to strive for perfection and excellence. Comăneci's performance contributed to a surge in interest and participation in gymnastics globally, particularly among young women.

3. Influence on Gymnastics Scoring and Judging: The historic nature of Comăneci's performance led to changes in how gymnastics scoring and judging were approached. Her perfect 10 prompted a reevaluation of the scoring system, leading to increased emphasis on precision and technical execution. The impact of her performance contributed to ongoing developments in the sport's rules and regulations.

4. Cultural and International Impact: Comăneci's achievement brought international attention to gymnastics and elevated the profile of the sport. Her success at the 1976 Olympics contributed to a greater appreciation for gymnastics as a competitive sport and showcased the skill and artistry involved. Comăneci's performance also played a role in increasing the visibility of Eastern European athletes in the global sports arena.

5. Legacy in the Sport: Nadia Comăneci's perfect 10 remains one of the most celebrated moments in Olympic history. Her achievement is often cited in discussions about the greatest moments in sports, and her name is synonymous with excellence in gymnastics. Comăneci's influence continues to be felt in the sport, as gymnasts and fans alike recognize her contributions to the evolution of gymnastics.

6. Enduring Popularity: Comăneci's performance at the 1976 Olympics has been commemorated and celebrated through various media and cultural references. Her story has been the

subject of documentaries, books, and films, highlighting her impact on gymnastics and her enduring legacy as one of the sport's greatest athletes.

Conclusion:

Nadia Comăneci's perfect 10 at the 1976 Montreal Olympics represents a defining moment in gymnastics history. Her flawless performance set a new standard for the sport, inspired future generations of gymnasts, and brought global attention to the artistry and precision of gymnastics. Comăneci's achievement remains a symbol of excellence and continues to be celebrated as one of the most iconic moments in Olympic history.

Miracle on Ice (1980)

The Historic Event:

On February 22, 1980, during the Winter Olympics held in Lake Placid, New York, the U.S. ice hockey team achieved one of the most remarkable upsets in sports history by defeating the Soviet Union 4-3 in a match that would become known as the "Miracle on Ice." This victory was not only a significant sporting achievement but also carried profound cultural and political implications during the Cold War era.

Context and Background:

1. Cold War Tensions: The "Miracle on Ice" occurred during a period of heightened Cold War tensions between the United States and the Soviet Union. The political climate was marked by rivalry and competition, and international sports events were often seen through the lens of these geopolitical struggles. The Soviet Union's dominance in ice hockey was

emblematic of its broader dominance in sports, which was used as a tool for propaganda and national pride.

2. U.S. Team Composition: The U.S. ice hockey team, composed primarily of amateur players and college athletes, was considered an underdog in the tournament. The team was led by coach Herb Brooks and included players such as Mike Eruzione, Jim Craig, and Mark Johnson. The team had been relatively inexperienced compared to the seasoned Soviet squad, which had been the gold medalist in the previous four Olympics and was widely regarded as the best hockey team in the world.

The Game:

1. The Match's Progress: The game was played at the Olympic Center in Lake Placid, and the Soviet team initially took a 2-1 lead. However, the U.S. team, demonstrating remarkable resilience and teamwork, fought back. Key moments included Mark Johnson's two goals and Mike Eruzione's decisive goal, which put the U.S. ahead 4-3. The U.S. team's goaltender, Jim Craig, delivered a series of crucial saves, especially during the final minutes of the game.

2. The Final Minutes: In the final moments of the game, with the Soviet team pressing hard for an equalizer, the U.S. defense held firm. The clock wound down to zero, and the U.S. team's 4-3 victory was secured, sending the crowd into euphoria.

Impact and Significance:

1. Cultural Impact: The "Miracle on Ice" was seen as a triumph of the underdog and a symbol of American perseverance and determination. The victory resonated with the American

public, who saw it as a symbol of hope and national pride amidst the tense political climate. The game is often cited as a defining moment in U.S. sports history, embodying the spirit of overcoming adversity and achieving the seemingly impossible.

2. Political Implications: The victory was more than just a sports achievement; it was a significant symbolic victory in the Cold War context. The U.S. team's win over the Soviet Union was perceived as a triumph over a geopolitical rival and served as a morale booster for the American public. It highlighted the idea of American exceptionalism and was celebrated as a moment of national unity.

3. Impact on Hockey: The "Miracle on Ice" brought increased attention to ice hockey in the United States. The game raised the profile of the sport, contributing to a growing interest in hockey at the amateur and professional levels. It also showcased the potential for amateur athletes to compete on the world stage and achieve remarkable success.

4. Legacy: The "Miracle on Ice" remains one of the most celebrated moments in Olympic history. The game is remembered for its dramatic intensity, the unexpected nature of the victory, and its impact on American sports culture. It has been commemorated in books, documentaries, and films, including the popular 2004 Disney movie "Miracle," which dramatizes the events surrounding the game.

5. Inspiration and National Pride: The victory inspired not only future generations of hockey players but also athletes across various sports. The "Miracle on Ice" is often cited as an example of how determination, teamwork, and belief in oneself can lead to extraordinary achievements. It remains a source of national pride and a reminder of the power of sports to unite and uplift.

Conclusion:

The "Miracle on Ice" is more than just a historic sports victory; it is a symbol of triumph over adversity and an enduring moment of national pride. The U.S. hockey team's unexpected victory over the Soviet Union in the 1980 Winter Olympics captured the imagination of the American public and left a lasting legacy in the world of sports. The game's cultural, political, and emotional significance continues to resonate, making it one of the greatest moments in Olympic history.

Usain Bolt's 9.58 Seconds (2009)

The Historic Achievement:

On August 16, 2009, at the World Athletics Championships in Berlin, Usain Bolt of Jamaica set a world record in the 100 meters with a time of 9.58 seconds. This remarkable performance solidified Bolt's status as the fastest man on earth and became one of the most iconic moments in athletics history.

Context and Background:

1. Bolt's Career Leading Up to 2009: By 2009, Usain Bolt had already established himself as a formidable sprinter. He had won gold medals in the 100 meters and 200 meters at the 2008 Beijing Olympics, where he set world records in both events. His performances were characterized by his explosive speed, unique running style, and charismatic personality, which endeared him to fans worldwide.

2. 2009 World Championships: The 2009 World Athletics Championships in Berlin was a significant event for Bolt. The competition was held at the Olympiastadion, a venue with a rich history of athletics. Bolt was the reigning Olympic champion and world record holder, and expectations were high for him to deliver another stellar performance.

The Race:

1. Bolt's Performance: In the 100 meters final, Bolt delivered a breathtaking performance, finishing in a world record time of 9.58 seconds. His start was relatively average, but he quickly accelerated to top speed and displayed an impressive combination of power and efficiency. Bolt's performance was marked by his characteristic stride and upright running form, which allowed him to cover ground with remarkable speed.

2. Key Moments: Bolt's race was notable for several reasons:

○ Dominance: Bolt's victory was achieved with a significant margin over his competitors, demonstrating his dominance in the event.

○ Reaction Time: Bolt's reaction time at the start of the race was 0.146 seconds, which was not particularly fast compared to other sprinters, but his top-end speed more than compensated for it.

○ Celebration: Bolt famously struck his signature "To the World" pose as he crossed the finish line, showcasing his confidence and adding to the spectacle of the moment.

Impact and Significance:

1. World Record Achievement: Bolt's 9.58-second time was a new world record, surpassing his previous record of 9.69 seconds set at the 2008 Beijing Olympics. The record shattered the previous benchmark and was widely regarded as an extraordinary achievement in the history of sprinting.

2. Bolt's Legacy: Usain Bolt's 9.58 seconds cemented his legacy as one of the greatest sprinters of all time. His combination of speed, technique, and showmanship set him apart from his

peers and established him as a global sports icon. Bolt's performances have inspired countless athletes and fans, highlighting the possibilities of human athleticism.

3. Impact on Athletics: Bolt's record had a profound impact on the sport of athletics. It set a new standard for sprinting and challenged future athletes to reach new heights. His performances contributed to the growing popularity of track and field and increased interest in sprinting events.

4. Global Recognition: Bolt's achievement garnered worldwide attention and praise. His charismatic personality, combined with his record-breaking performances, made him a household name. Bolt received numerous accolades and awards, including being named the IAAF World Athlete of the Year and receiving the Laureus World Sportsman of the Year award.

5. Enduring Popularity: Usain Bolt's 9.58-second record remains one of the most celebrated moments in sports history. His race in Berlin is frequently cited as a benchmark for excellence in sprinting and continues to be referenced in discussions about the greatest athletic achievements. Bolt's legacy as the fastest man on earth endures, and his impact on the sport of athletics is widely recognized.

Conclusion:

Usain Bolt's 9.58-second 100 meters at the 2009 World Championships in Berlin is a defining moment in the history of athletics. Bolt's record-breaking performance solidified his status as the fastest man on earth and showcased the pinnacle of human speed and athleticism. The achievement remains a symbol of excellence in sprinting and continues to inspire athletes and fans around the world. Bolt's legacy as a sports icon and his contribution to the sport of athletics are celebrated through his historic run and enduring influence.

Chapter 4: Basketball's Finest Moments

<u>Wilt Chamberlain's 100-Point Game (1962)</u>

The Historic Achievement:

On March 2, 1962, Wilt Chamberlain of the Philadelphia Warriors scored 100 points in a single NBA game against the New York Knicks. This remarkable feat remains the highest-scoring performance in the history of the NBA and is one of the most iconic moments in basketball history.

Context and Background:

1. Chamberlain's Career: Wilt Chamberlain was a dominant force in professional basketball, known for his exceptional scoring ability, size, and athleticism. By 1962, he had already established himself as one of the most prolific players in the league, having won the NBA scoring title multiple times and earning accolades for his remarkable performances on the court.

2. The 1961-1962 NBA Season: The 1961-1962 NBA season was notable for Chamberlain's outstanding individual performances. He led the league in scoring, rebounding, and assists, showcasing his versatility and impact on the game. His 100-point game was the culmination of an extraordinary season in which he averaged 50.4 points per game.

The Game:

1. Details of the Performance:

o Location: The game took place at the Hershey Sports Arena in Hershey, Pennsylvania. The venue was relatively small, with a seating capacity of around 8,000, which provided an intimate setting for Chamberlain's historic performance.

○ Scoring: Chamberlain's 100-point game was achieved through a combination of field goals, free throws, and remarkable consistency. He made 36 of 63 field goal attempts and 28 of 32 free throw attempts. His performance included a wide range of shots, from close-range layups to mid-range jumpers.

○ Recording and Broadcast: The game was not televised, and there is no known audio recording of Chamberlain's historic performance. The only available footage is from a brief highlight reel and post-game interviews. The official box score and reports from newspapers provide documentation of the feat.

2. Key Moments:

○ Scoring Spree: Chamberlain's scoring spree was marked by periods of intense offensive play. He scored 41 points in the first half and continued his remarkable performance in the second half, eventually reaching the 100-point milestone.

○ Final Moments: Chamberlain's achievement was met with excitement and disbelief from his teammates and spectators. The game ended with the Warriors defeating the Knicks 169-147, and Chamberlain's 100 points were celebrated as an extraordinary accomplishment.

Impact and Significance:

1. Unmatched Feat: Wilt Chamberlain's 100-point game remains an unmatched feat in NBA history. No player has

come close to reaching this milestone, making it a unique and enduring record. The achievement is often cited as the pinnacle of individual scoring in professional basketball.

2. Legacy of Chamberlain: Chamberlain's 100-point game solidified his status as one of the greatest players in basketball history. His dominance on the court, coupled with this extraordinary performance, contributed to his legacy as a basketball icon. Chamberlain's impact on the game is remembered through his scoring records and his influence on future generations of players.

3. Cultural Impact: The 100-point game has become a part of basketball lore and is frequently referenced in discussions about the greatest moments in sports history. Chamberlain's accomplishment is celebrated in books, documentaries, and media coverage, highlighting its significance in the annals of sports history.

4. Challenges and Criticisms: While Chamberlain's 100-point game is celebrated, it has also faced some criticism and skepticism. Some critics argue that the achievement was aided by the relatively small venue and the fact that the game was played in an era with different rules and playing conditions compared to the modern game.

5. Enduring Legacy: Despite any criticisms, Wilt Chamberlain's 100-point game remains an enduring symbol of individual excellence and achievement in basketball. The record continues to inspire players and fans, and Chamberlain's legacy is celebrated through the continued recognition of this historic performance.

Conclusion:

Wilt Chamberlain's 100-point game on March 2, 1962, is a defining moment in NBA history and a testament to individual athletic excellence. The achievement stands as the highest-scoring performance in the history of professional basketball and continues to be a celebrated and iconic moment in sports. Chamberlain's accomplishment not only highlights his exceptional talent and skill but also serves as a lasting symbol of the extraordinary possibilities within the game of basketball.

Michael Jordan's "Flu Game" (1997)

The Historic Performance:

On June 11, 1997, during Game 5 of the NBA Finals between the Chicago Bulls and the Utah Jazz, Michael Jordan delivered one of the most memorable performances in basketball history despite being severely ill. This game, often referred to as the "Flu Game," showcased Jordan's incredible resilience and skill under extreme conditions and played a crucial role in the Bulls' quest for their fifth NBA championship.

Context and Background:

1. The 1997 NBA Finals: The Chicago Bulls, led by Michael Jordan, were facing the Utah Jazz in the 1997 NBA Finals. The series was highly competitive, and both teams were vying for the championship. The Bulls had won three consecutive NBA titles from 1991 to 1993 and were seeking to reclaim their dominance after Jordan's brief retirement and return to the league.

2. Jordan's Illness: Jordan's performance in Game 5 was remarkable due to the severe illness he was battling. Reports suggest that Jordan was suffering from flu-like symptoms, which included high fever, fatigue, and dehydration. The exact nature of his illness remains debated, with some speculating that it may have been food poisoning rather than the flu.

The Game:

1. Jordan's Performance:

o Stats: Despite his illness, Jordan played 44 minutes and scored 38 points, including 7 rebounds, 5 assists, and 3 steals. His performance was characterized by his ability to make crucial shots, including a three-pointer with less than a minute remaining that helped secure the Bulls' victory.

o Key Moments: Jordan's most iconic moment of the game came with his three-pointer in the closing moments, which gave the Bulls a decisive lead. His clutch performance, despite his physical condition, was instrumental in the Bulls' 90-88 victory over the Jazz.

2. Visuals and Impact:

o Physical Condition: Jordan was visibly exhausted and struggling during the game, often leaning on teammates or sitting on the bench during timeouts. His condition was a dramatic contrast to his typically energetic and dominant presence on the court.

o Teammates' Support: Teammates, including Scottie Pippen and Steve Kerr, played a crucial role in supporting Jordan. Pippen, in particular, contributed significantly with 17 points and 10 rebounds, helping to alleviate some of the pressure on Jordan.

Impact and Significance:

1. Myth and Legacy: The "Flu Game" has become a legendary part of Michael Jordan's mythology, symbolizing his toughness, determination, and clutch performance under

adversity. The game is frequently cited as an example of Jordan's unparalleled competitive spirit and his ability to deliver in high-pressure situations.

2. Cultural Impact: The "Flu Game" has become an iconic moment in sports culture, often referenced in discussions about Jordan's greatness. It is celebrated as one of the defining performances of Jordan's career and a testament to his ability to overcome obstacles and perform at the highest level.

3. Criticisms and Clarifications: Some critics have questioned the extent of Jordan's illness and the true nature of his condition. While many view the performance as a heroic effort, others suggest that the illness may have been exaggerated or that Jordan's performance should be viewed in the context of the era's physical and mental demands on athletes.

4. Historical Significance: The "Flu Game" was a pivotal moment in the 1997 NBA Finals, contributing to the Bulls' 90-88 victory and helping them secure a 3-2 series lead. The Bulls went on to win the championship in Game 6, adding to Jordan's legacy as a champion and clutch performer.

5. Enduring Legacy: Michael Jordan's "Flu Game" remains one of the most memorable and celebrated performances in NBA history. The game is often highlighted as a symbol of Jordan's greatness and has been featured in documentaries, books, and media coverage, further cementing its place in sports lore.

Conclusion:

Michael Jordan's "Flu Game" of the 1997 NBA Finals stands as a testament to his extraordinary skill, resilience, and competitive spirit. Despite battling severe illness, Jordan delivered a performance that showcased his ability to perform at the highest level under adverse conditions. The game remains a defining moment in Jordan's illustrious career and a celebrated example of sports excellence and determination.

The 1992 Dream Team

The Historic Assembly:

The 1992 Dream Team is widely considered the greatest basketball team ever assembled. Composed of NBA superstars and hall-of-famers, the team represented the United States in the Barcelona Olympics and dominated the competition, fundamentally changing the global landscape of basketball.

Context and Background:

1. Preceding Context:

o U.S. Basketball History: Prior to 1992, the U.S. men's basketball team had used collegiate players (often referred to as the "Amateur" teams) in Olympic competitions. However, the U.S. lost to the Soviet Union in the 1972 Olympics and the competition in international basketball was intensifying.

o Rise of Global Basketball: The 1980s saw the rise of international basketball talent, with countries like the Soviet Union, Spain, and Argentina becoming increasingly competitive. This prompted the U.S. to consider a new strategy for assembling its Olympic team.

2. The Decision to Include NBA Players:

o The 1991 FIBA World Championships: The U.S. team's loss in the 1988 Seoul Olympics and subsequent struggles in international competitions led to the decision to field a team composed of NBA professionals. The idea was to assemble the best possible roster to reclaim dominance in international basketball.

The Dream Team:

1. Roster and Players: The Dream Team was comprised of the following players:

○ Michael Jordan (Chicago Bulls) - Often considered the greatest player of all time, Jordan was the team's leader and primary scorer.

○ Magic Johnson (Los Angeles Lakers) - A legendary point guard known for his playmaking and leadership.

○ Larry Bird (Boston Celtics) - Renowned for his shooting, passing, and basketball IQ.

○ Charles Barkley (Phoenix Suns) - A dominant forward known for his scoring and rebounding.

○ Scottie Pippen (Chicago Bulls) - A versatile forward and defensive specialist.

○ David Robinson (San Antonio Spurs) - A dominant center known for his defensive prowess.

○ Patrick Ewing (New York Knicks) - An imposing center with strong scoring and rebounding skills.

○ John Stockton (Utah Jazz) - The NBA's all-time leader in assists and steals, known for his precise passing.

○ Clyde Drexler (Portland Trail Blazers) - An explosive shooting guard known for his athleticism and scoring ability.

○ Christian Laettner (Duke University) - The only college player selected, known for his versatility and skill.

○ Bob Knight (Head Coach) - A highly respected college coach known for his disciplined approach and success with Indiana University.

2. Preparation and Training:

○ Training Camp: The team's preparation included a series of practices and exhibition games against NBA teams and international opponents. The practices were highly competitive, and the team's unity and chemistry quickly developed.

○ Exhibition Games: The Dream Team played several exhibition games leading up to the Olympics, including matches against NBA teams and international squads. These games demonstrated the team's dominance and provided a glimpse of the incredible talent and teamwork on display.

The Olympics:
1. Dominance in Barcelona:

○ Group Stage: The Dream Team won all their games in the preliminary round with overwhelming margins, showcasing their superior skill and athleticism.

○ Knockout Rounds: The team continued their dominant performance in the knockout stages, defeating opponents with significant leads and demonstrating a high level of play.

2. Impact and Cultural Significance:

○ Global Exposure: The Dream Team's dominance and style of play captivated audiences worldwide, significantly raising the profile of basketball on the international stage. The team's performance contributed to a surge in global interest in the NBA and basketball in general.

○ Inspiration: The Dream Team inspired a generation of young basketball players around the world. The visibility and success of the team helped to popularize the sport and encouraged the development of talent in countries outside the U.S.

○ Legacy: The Dream Team is often credited with elevating the global game of basketball, leading to the increased presence of NBA players in international competitions and fostering the growth of the sport.

Impact and Significance:
1. Transformation of International Basketball:

○ Increased Competition: The Dream Team's success highlighted the need for other nations to improve their basketball programs. It spurred many countries to invest in their basketball development and compete at higher levels.

○ NBA Globalization: The Dream Team played a crucial role in the globalization of the NBA, leading to a greater international presence in the league and expanding its fan base globally.

2. Enduring Legacy:

○ Historical Achievement: The 1992 Dream Team is celebrated as one of the greatest assemblages of basketball talent ever. The team's performance remains a benchmark for excellence in international basketball and is frequently referenced in discussions about the greatest sports teams of all time.

○ Continued Influence: The Dream Team's impact continues to be felt in the sport today, with international players becoming an integral part of the NBA and global basketball competitions.

Conclusion:

The 1992 Dream Team's assembly and dominance in the Barcelona Olympics represent a transformative moment in sports history. The team's unparalleled talent, dominant performances, and global impact have cemented its legacy as the greatest basketball team ever. The Dream Team's success not only reasserted the U.S. dominance in basketball but also revolutionized the sport on a global scale, inspiring future generations and expanding the reach of the game.

Chapter 5: Football Feats

<u>The "Immaculate Reception" (1972)</u>

The Historic Play:

The "Immaculate Reception" is one of the most iconic and controversial plays in NFL history. It occurred on December 23, 1972, during an AFC Divisional Playoff game between the Pittsburgh Steelers and the Oakland Raiders. Franco Harris's miraculous catch and subsequent run led to a game-winning touchdown, becoming a defining moment in NFL folklore.

Context and Background:

1. The 1972 NFL Season:

   o Steelers' Rise: The 1972 season was pivotal for the Pittsburgh Steelers, who were starting to emerge as a competitive team under the leadership of head coach Chuck Noll. The team had struggled in previous seasons but was showing signs of improvement.

   o Raiders' Dominance: The Oakland Raiders, led by head coach John Madden, were one of the most formidable teams of the era. They had a strong defense and were considered a dominant force in the league.

2. The Game Situation:

   o AFC Divisional Playoff: The game was a critical playoff match, with the winner advancing to the AFC Championship. The stakes were high, and both teams were fighting fiercely for a chance to continue their championship pursuit.

○ Score and Time: With less than a minute left in the game, the Raiders were leading 7-6. The Steelers faced a 4th-and-10 situation on their own 40-yard line, making the game's final moments highly tense and uncertain.

The Play:

1. Description of the Play:

○ The Pass: On the final play of the game, Steelers quarterback Terry Bradshaw threw a deep pass toward the middle of the field. The pass was intended for running back John "Frenchy" Fuqua, who was being closely guarded by Raiders safety Jack Tatum.

○ The Catch: The ball appeared to be deflected by Tatum, and in a miraculous turn of events, Franco Harris, the Steelers' running back, caught the deflected ball just inches off the ground. Harris then ran the ball into the end zone for a 60-yard touchdown.

○ Controversy: The play was immediately controversial, as there were questions about whether the ball had touched the ground or if Fuqua had been the first player to touch the ball. The officials ruled it a legal catch, and the touchdown stood, giving the Steelers a 13-7 victory.

2. Key Moments:

○ Immediate Reactions: The play was met with disbelief and excitement from the Steelers' players and fans, while the Raiders' players and supporters were left stunned and frustrated. The controversial nature of the play added to its mystique and significance.

o Aftermath: The touchdown secured the Steelers' victory and advanced them to the AFC Championship. The Steelers eventually went on to win Super Bowl IX, marking the beginning of their dynasty in the 1970s.

Impact and Significance:
1. NFL Folklore:

o Iconic Status: The "Immaculate Reception" has become one of the most celebrated and debated plays in NFL history. It is frequently referenced in discussions about the greatest moments in football and is considered a defining play of the sport.

o Media Coverage: The play has been featured in numerous highlight reels, documentaries, and retrospectives, solidifying its place in NFL folklore. The dramatic and controversial nature of the play has contributed to its enduring legacy.

2. Cultural Impact:

o Steelers' Legacy: The play is credited with helping to establish the Pittsburgh Steelers as a dominant team in the NFL. The victory in the 1972 playoff game was a significant milestone in the team's history and contributed to their eventual success in the 1970s.

o Fan Connection: The "Immaculate Reception" is a cherished moment for Steelers fans and is often cited as a symbol of the team's resilience and ability to achieve the seemingly impossible. It has become an integral part of the team's identity and fan culture.

3. Controversy and Debate:

○ Rules and Interpretations: The play has been the subject of ongoing debate regarding the rules and interpretations of the catch. While the officials' ruling stands, discussions about the legality of the play continue to fuel interest and analysis.

○ Raiders' Perspective: The Raiders and their supporters view the play as a controversial and unfair decision, adding to the rivalry between the two teams and contributing to the play's mystique.

4. Enduring Legacy:

○ Historical Significance: The "Immaculate Reception" remains a defining moment in NFL history and is frequently highlighted in discussions about the greatest plays of all time. It is celebrated for its dramatic execution and impact on the course of the game.

○ Cultural Impact: The play has influenced the way memorable moments in sports are remembered and celebrated. It continues to be a symbol of excitement, controversy, and the unpredictability of football.

Conclusion:

The "Immaculate Reception" of 1972 stands as one of the most iconic and controversial plays in NFL history. Franco Harris's miraculous catch and touchdown epitomize the drama and excitement of professional football, and the play's enduring legacy is a testament to its significance in the sport's history. The play not only secured a crucial victory for the Pittsburgh Steelers but also cemented its place in

NFL folklore as a moment of incredible athleticism, controversy, and unforgettable drama.

Joe Montana's 92-Yard Drive (1989)

The Historic Drive:

Joe Montana's 92-yard drive in Super Bowl XXIII is often hailed as one of the greatest moments in NFL history. This drive, which culminated in a game-winning touchdown, exemplifies Montana's composure, precision, and greatness as a quarterback under the highest-pressure circumstances.

Context and Background:

1. The 1988 NFL Season:

○ San Francisco 49ers: The San Francisco 49ers, led by head coach Bill Walsh and quarterback Joe Montana, had a highly successful season in 1988. They finished with a 10-6 record and advanced to the playoffs as one of the top teams in the NFC.

○ Cincinnati Bengals: The Cincinnati Bengals, led by head coach Sam Wyche and quarterback Boomer Esiason, also had a strong season, finishing with a 12-4 record. They were making their first Super Bowl appearance and were seen as a formidable opponent.

2. Super Bowl XXIII:

○ Date and Venue: Super Bowl XXIII took place on January 22, 1989, at Joe Robbie Stadium in Miami, Florida. The game was highly anticipated, featuring two strong teams with talented rosters.

○ Score and Situation: The Bengals led the game 16-13 with just over three minutes remaining in the fourth quarter. The 49ers had possession of the ball, but they were starting their drive from their own 8-yard line, facing a challenging situation.

The Drive:
1. Description of the Drive:

○ Starting Point: The 49ers began their drive with 3:20 remaining on the clock, deep in their own territory at the 8-yard line.

○ Key Plays: Montana demonstrated exceptional poise and precision throughout the drive. He made several crucial completions, including a 15-yard pass to Jerry Rice and a 10-yard pass to Roger Craig. The drive also featured a pivotal 25-yard completion to tight end John Taylor.

○ The Touchdown: With 34 seconds left in the game, Montana completed a 10-yard touchdown pass to John Taylor in the end zone, giving the 49ers a 20-16 lead. The Bengals were unable to respond, and the 49ers secured the victory.

2. Key Moments:

○ Montana's Composure: Montana's ability to remain calm and execute the drive with precision under immense pressure was a testament to his greatness as a quarterback. His leadership and decision-making were critical in the game's final moments.

○ The Winning Touchdown: The touchdown pass to Taylor was a perfectly timed and executed play that exemplified Montana's clutch performance and the 49ers' offensive prowess.

Impact and Significance:
1. Joe Montana's Legacy:

○ Super Bowl Greatness: The drive solidified Joe Montana's reputation as one of the greatest quarterbacks in NFL history. His ability to perform under pressure and lead his team to victory in critical moments became a defining characteristic of his career.

○ Four Super Bowl Wins: Montana's performance in Super Bowl XXIII was one of four Super Bowl victories he led the 49ers to during his career. His success in the postseason and ability to deliver in high-stakes situations contributed to his legendary status.

2. The 49ers' Legacy:

○ Dynasty: The victory in Super Bowl XXIII was part of the 49ers' dominant run in the late 1980s and early 1990s. The team's success, including three Super Bowl victories in four years, established them as one of the NFL's premier franchises.

○ Coaching Influence: Head coach Bill Walsh's innovative offensive strategies and emphasis on precision passing were instrumental in the 49ers' success. The drive highlighted the effectiveness of Walsh's offensive system and its impact on the game.

3. Cultural Impact:

○ Iconic Moment: Joe Montana's 92-yard drive has become an iconic moment in NFL history, often cited in discussions about the greatest plays and performances in Super Bowl history. The drive is frequently featured in highlight reels and retrospectives.

○ Inspiration: The drive has served as an inspiration for future generations of quarterbacks and football players. Montana's performance exemplifies the qualities of leadership, composure, and excellence that are celebrated in the sport.

Enduring Legacy:
1. Historical Significance:

○ Super Bowl XXIII's Status: The drive is remembered as one of the most dramatic and significant moments in Super Bowl history. It exemplified the high level of competition and excitement that defines the NFL's championship game.

○ Montana's Performance: The drive is a key highlight of Joe Montana's illustrious career and is often referenced in discussions about his place among the greatest quarterbacks of all time.

2. Continued Recognition:

○ NFL Highlights: The 92-yard drive is a staple of NFL highlight reels and is frequently discussed in media coverage of Super Bowl moments. Montana's performance continues to be celebrated as a defining moment of his career and the 49ers' success.

Conclusion:

Joe Montana's 92-yard drive in Super Bowl XXIII stands as a defining moment in NFL history, showcasing Montana's exceptional skill, leadership, and ability to perform under pressure. The drive not only secured the 49ers' victory in the Super Bowl but also cemented Montana's legacy as one of the greatest quarterbacks of all time. The drive remains an iconic and celebrated moment in sports history, embodying the drama, excitement, and excellence of the NFL's championship game.

New England Patriots' Super Bowl LI Comeback (2017)

The Historic Comeback:

The New England Patriots' comeback in Super Bowl LI (51) is widely regarded as the greatest comeback in Super Bowl history. Trailing by 28-3 in the third quarter, the Patriots rallied to defeat the Atlanta Falcons 34-28 in overtime, showcasing remarkable resilience, strategy, and execution.

Context and Background:

1. The 2016 NFL Season:

○ Patriots' Performance: The New England Patriots, led by head coach Bill Belichick and quarterback Tom Brady, finished the 2016 regular season with a 14-2 record, the best in the NFL. They were a dominant force throughout the season and entered the playoffs as the top seed in the AFC.

○ Falcons' Performance: The Atlanta Falcons, under head coach Dan Quinn and quarterback Matt Ryan, had a stellar season, finishing with an 11-5 record. They were known for their high-powered offense and had a strong defensive unit.

2. Super Bowl LI:

○ Date and Venue: Super Bowl LI took place on February 5, 2017, at NRG Stadium in Houston, Texas. The game featured the New England Patriots representing the AFC and the Atlanta Falcons representing the NFC.

○ Score and Situation: The Falcons held a commanding 28-3 lead with 2:08 left in the third quarter. The Patriots faced a significant challenge as they needed to overcome a 25-point deficit to secure victory.

The Comeback:
1. The Patriots' Rally:

○ Scoring Surge: The Patriots began their comeback with a 5-yard touchdown pass from Tom Brady to running back James White. This was followed by a 2-point conversion, narrowing the deficit to 28-11.

○ Key Plays: The Patriots continued their offensive surge with a 1-yard touchdown run by James White and a 2-point conversion to make it 28-20. The defense also played a crucial role, with a key stop against the Falcons' offense.

○ Tying the Game: With 57 seconds left in regulation, Tom Brady connected with wide receiver Julian Edelman for a 6-yard touchdown pass. The Patriots successfully converted a 2-point attempt to tie the game 28-28, sending it into overtime.

2. The Overtime Victory:

○ Overtime Rules: The game went into overtime, with the Patriots winning the coin toss and receiving the ball first.

○ Game-Winning Drive: The Patriots methodically moved down the field, capping off their drive with a 2-yard touchdown run by James White. The touchdown secured a 34-28 victory, completing the greatest comeback in Super Bowl history.

Impact and Significance:
1. Tom Brady's Legacy:

○ Historic Performance: The comeback solidified Tom Brady's reputation as one of the greatest quarterbacks in NFL history. His performance in Super Bowl LI, including leading the largest comeback in Super Bowl history, added to his legacy as a clutch performer.

○ Fifth Super Bowl Win: The victory in Super Bowl LI was Brady's fifth Super Bowl win, further establishing him as one of the most successful quarterbacks in NFL history.

2. Patriots' Legacy:

○ Dynasty: The win in Super Bowl LI was a key moment in the New England Patriots' dynasty under Bill Belichick and Tom Brady. The Patriots' success in the 2000s and 2010s, including their Super Bowl LI victory, contributed to their status as one of the NFL's premier franchises.

○ Comeback Culture: The game demonstrated the Patriots' ability to perform under pressure and their resilience in overcoming significant challenges. The comeback became a defining moment in the team's history and a testament to their competitive spirit.

3. Cultural Impact:

○ Iconic Moment: The comeback is celebrated as one of the most dramatic and memorable moments in Super Bowl history. It is frequently cited in discussions about the greatest games and comebacks in NFL history.

○ Inspiration: The Patriots' rally has served as an inspiration for teams and athletes in various sports. It exemplifies the importance of perseverance, strategy, and execution in overcoming seemingly insurmountable odds.

4. Historical Significance:

○ Super Bowl LI's Status: The comeback in Super Bowl LI is recognized as the largest deficit overcome in Super Bowl history. It is a historic achievement that is often highlighted in discussions about the greatest moments in NFL history.

○ Enduring Legacy: The game remains a significant part of NFL lore, celebrated for its dramatic twists, high-stakes excitement, and the remarkable performance of the Patriots and Tom Brady.

Conclusion:

The New England Patriots' comeback in Super Bowl LI stands as a defining moment in NFL history, showcasing the team's resilience, strategy, and execution under pressure. The game highlighted Tom Brady's greatness as a quarterback and solidified the Patriots' legacy as one of the NFL's premier franchises. The comeback is celebrated as the greatest in Super Bowl history and continues to inspire and captivate fans and athletes alike.

Chapter 6: Iconic World Cup Moments

Pelé's 1,000th Goal (1969)

The Milestone:

Pelé's 1,000th goal in professional soccer, achieved on November 19, 1969, is one of the most celebrated moments in the sport's history. This milestone not only highlighted Pelé's extraordinary skill and consistency but also cemented his status as one of the greatest soccer players of all time.

Context and Background:

1. Pelé's Career:

○ Early Success: Pelé, born Edson Arantes do Nascimento, began his professional career at the age of 15 with Santos FC in Brazil. By the time he reached his 1,000th goal, he had already established himself as a dominant force in soccer, with multiple domestic and international titles.

○ Achievements: Pelé had won several titles with Santos, including the São Paulo State Championship and the Copa Libertadores. He had also earned international acclaim with the Brazilian national team, winning three FIFA World Cups (1958, 1962, and 1970).

2. The Road to 1,000 Goals:

○ Scoring Record: Pelé's journey to 1,000 goals was marked by his prolific scoring ability and versatility on the field. He scored goals in domestic league matches, cup competitions, and international games, showcasing his exceptional talent and consistency.

○ Approaching the Milestone: By 1969, Pelé was approaching the landmark of 1,000 career goals. The anticipation grew as he closed in on the historic achievement.

The 1,000th Goal:
1. The Game:

○ Date and Venue: Pelé scored his 1,000th goal on November 19, 1969, during a match between Santos FC and Vasco da Gama at the Maracanã Stadium in Rio de Janeiro, Brazil.

○ The Goal: Pelé's milestone goal came in the 32nd minute of the match. It was a penalty kick, a fitting way to mark such a historic achievement. The goal was celebrated with a grand display of fan enthusiasm and media coverage.

2. Celebration:

○ Public Reaction: The scoring of Pelé's 1,000th goal was met with widespread celebration and recognition. The event was marked by a large crowd, a festive atmosphere, and numerous tributes to Pelé's incredible achievement.

○ Ceremony: The game was interrupted briefly for a special ceremony to honor Pelé. He was presented with a commemorative plaque and celebrated by his teammates, fans, and dignitaries.

Impact and Significance:

1. Pelé's Legacy:

o Record Achievement: Scoring 1,000 goals in professional soccer is an extraordinary achievement that underscores Pelé's exceptional skill, consistency, and longevity in the sport. It highlighted his place among the greatest soccer players of all time.

o Influence: Pelé's accomplishment contributed to his legendary status and inspired future generations of soccer players. His scoring prowess, sportsmanship, and impact on the game have been widely recognized and celebrated.

2. Soccer's History:

o Historical Milestone: Pelé's 1,000th goal is a landmark moment in soccer history, celebrated for its significance and the context in which it was achieved. It is often referenced in discussions about the greatest achievements in the sport.

o Cultural Impact: The milestone reinforced soccer's global appeal and Pelé's role in popularizing the sport. It highlighted the excitement and passion associated with soccer and contributed to the sport's growth and development.

3. Cultural Impact:

o Iconic Status: Pelé's 1,000th goal is an iconic moment that continues to be remembered and celebrated in soccer culture. It is featured in retrospectives and historical accounts of the sport's most significant achievements.

○ Legacy: The goal is a testament to Pelé's enduring legacy and his impact on the sport. It serves as a symbol of excellence and achievement in soccer, inspiring players and fans around the world.

Conclusion:

Pelé's 1,000th goal in 1969 is a defining moment in the history of soccer, showcasing his extraordinary talent and cementing his place among the sport's greatest legends. The milestone goal not only celebrated Pelé's remarkable career but also highlighted the excitement and global appeal of soccer. The achievement remains a significant part of soccer lore and continues to inspire and captivate fans and players.

<u>Diego Maradona's "Hand of God" and "Goal of the Century" (1986)</u>

The 1986 World Cup Quarterfinal:

Diego Maradona's performance in the 1986 FIFA World Cup quarterfinal match between Argentina and England on June 22, 1986, is one of the most memorable and controversial in soccer history. The match featured two iconic moments: the "Hand of God" goal and the "Goal of the Century," both of which had a profound impact on the game and on Maradona's legendary status.

Context and Background:

1. The 1986 FIFA World Cup:

○ Location and Significance: The 1986 World Cup was held in Mexico, and it was a highly anticipated tournament featuring many of the world's best teams and players. Argentina, led by Diego Maradona, was a strong contender, while England was also a formidable team.

○ Argentina's Journey: Argentina, under the management of Carlos Bilardo, had a strong squad and was looking to win their second World Cup. Maradona, who was in exceptional form, was the team's captain and key player.

2. The England-Argentina Match:

○ Date and Venue: The match took place on June 22, 1986, at the Estadio Azteca in Mexico City, one of the most famous soccer stadiums in the world.

○ The Stakes: The winner of the quarterfinal match would advance to the semifinals, making it a high-stakes game with significant implications for both teams.

The Moments:
1. The "Hand of God" Goal:

○ Description: In the 51st minute of the match, Maradona used his left hand to punch the ball into the net, which was subsequently awarded as a goal by the referee. The use of his hand was against the rules, but it went unnoticed by the officials.

○ Controversy: The goal was highly controversial and sparked outrage among English players and fans, who felt that Maradona had cheated. Maradona later famously described the goal as "a little bit with my head, and a little bit with the hand of God."

○ Impact: The "Hand of God" goal gave Argentina a 1-0 lead. Despite the controversy, it was a pivotal moment in the match.

○

2. The "Goal of the Century":

○ Description: Just minutes after the controversial goal, in the 55th minute, Maradona scored what is often regarded as one of the greatest goals in World Cup history. He dribbled past five England players from his own half of the field, showcasing extraordinary skill, control, and speed.

○ Execution: Maradona's run from the halfway line, his ability to navigate through the English defense, and his precise finish past goalkeeper Peter Shilton were nothing short of spectacular. The goal was celebrated for its brilliance and technical excellence.

○ Impact: The "Goal of the Century" extended Argentina's lead to 2-0 and is widely considered one of the greatest goals in World Cup history. It solidified Maradona's status as one of soccer's greatest players.

Impact and Significance:
1. Diego Maradona's Legacy:

○ Legendary Status: The two goals in this match cemented Maradona's legacy as one of the greatest soccer players of all time. The contrast between the controversial "Hand of God" goal and the extraordinary "Goal of the Century" highlighted his complex and dynamic personality.

○ World Cup Victory: Maradona's performances throughout the tournament, including these two goals, helped Argentina win the World Cup. He was named the tournament's best player and won the Golden Ball award.

2. Soccer History:

○ Iconic Moments: The "Hand of God" and "Goal of the Century" are among the most iconic moments in World Cup history. They are frequently referenced in discussions about the greatest games and performances in soccer.

○ Controversy and Brilliance: The contrast between the two goals underscores the dual nature of Maradona's legacy—marked by moments of controversy and brilliance.

3. Cultural Impact:

○ Global Recognition: The match and Maradona's goals gained global recognition and have been featured in countless retrospectives and highlight reels. The "Hand of God" and "Goal of the Century" remain essential parts of soccer lore.

○ Inspiration: Maradona's performance continues to inspire soccer players and fans. The "Goal of the Century" is celebrated as a model of individual skill and creativity, while the "Hand of God" reflects the complexities of competitive sports.

Conclusion:

Diego Maradona's "Hand of God" and "Goal of the Century" during the 1986 World Cup quarterfinal against England are two of the most memorable and debated moments in soccer history. The "Hand of God" showcased Maradona's controversial side, while the "Goal of the Century" highlighted his unparalleled skill and creativity. Together, these moments defined Maradona's World Cup performance and contributed to his enduring legacy as one of the sport's greatest players alike.

Cristiano Ronaldo's Bicycle Kick Goal (2018)

The Iconic Goal:

Cristiano Ronaldo's bicycle kick goal against Juventus in the UEFA Champions League quarterfinal match on April 3, 2018, is widely celebrated as one of the most spectacular goals in soccer history. This moment showcased Ronaldo's extraordinary skill, athleticism, and precision, solidifying his reputation as one of the greatest soccer players of all time.

Context and Background:

1. UEFA Champions League:

○ Tournament Significance: The UEFA Champions League is one of the most prestigious and competitive club tournaments in world soccer. Winning the Champions League is a major achievement for any player or club.

○ Real Madrid vs. Juventus: In the quarterfinal match, Real Madrid, where Cristiano Ronaldo was playing, faced Juventus, one of Italy's top teams. The game was highly anticipated due to the high profile of both teams and their key players.

2. Cristiano Ronaldo's Form:

○ Player Profile: Cristiano Ronaldo, known for his incredible scoring ability, speed, and physical prowess, was in top form during the 2017-2018 season. At this stage of his career, he had already won multiple Ballon d'Or awards and was a key player for both Real Madrid and the Portuguese national team.

○ Previous Achievements: Ronaldo had previously led Real Madrid to several Champions League titles and was known for his ability to deliver in crucial moments.

The Bicycle Kick Goal:
1. The Moment:

○ Date and Venue: The bicycle kick goal occurred on April 3, 2018, during the Champions League quarterfinal match between Real Madrid and Juventus at the Allianz Stadium in Turin, Italy.

○ Description: In the 64th minute of the match, Ronaldo leaped into the air and executed a flawless bicycle kick, striking the ball with his left foot while airborne. The ball flew past Juventus goalkeeper Gianluigi Buffon and into the top corner of the net.

2. Execution:

○ Technical Brilliance: The goal demonstrated Ronaldo's exceptional timing, balance, and technique. The precision and power of the strike left Buffon with no chance to save it. The goal was widely praised for its technical difficulty and beauty.

○ Reaction: Ronaldo's bicycle kick was met with astonishment from fans, players, and pundits. The goal was celebrated by Real Madrid supporters and acknowledged with respect by Juventus fans, despite its impact on their team.

Impact and Significance:
1. Cristiano Ronaldo's Legacy:

o Historical Achievement: The bicycle kick goal is considered one of the greatest goals in Champions League history and a defining moment in Ronaldo's illustrious career. It further cemented his status as one of soccer's greatest players.

o Recognition: Ronaldo's goal was recognized with widespread acclaim and is often featured in highlight reels and retrospectives of his career. It is celebrated for its aesthetic appeal and technical excellence.

2. Soccer History:

o Iconic Moment: The goal is frequently cited as one of the most memorable moments in the history of the UEFA Champions League. It stands out for its rarity and the level of skill required to execute such a move successfully.

o Influence: Ronaldo's bicycle kick demonstrated the beauty and excitement of soccer, inspiring players and fans around the world. It exemplified the skill and creativity that make soccer a captivating sport.

3. Cultural Impact:

o Global Celebration: The goal received global recognition and was widely covered by media and sports networks. It was celebrated as a moment of brilliance and athleticism.

o Enduring Image: The bicycle kick has become an iconic image associated with Ronaldo and Real Madrid. It is a symbol of the extraordinary achievements and moments that define the sport.

Conclusion:

Cristiano Ronaldo's bicycle kick goal against Juventus in the 2018 UEFA Champions League quarterfinal is a landmark moment in soccer history, showcasing the beauty, skill, and precision that define the sport. The goal not only highlighted Ronaldo's exceptional talent but also contributed to his legacy as one of the greatest players in soccer history. It remains an iconic moment that continues to inspire and captivate soccer fans and players around the world.

Chapter 7: Unstoppable Forces in Tennis

<u>Billie Jean King Defeats Bobby Riggs (1973)</u>

The Battle of the Sexes:

Billie Jean King's victory over Bobby Riggs in the "Battle of the Sexes" tennis match on September 20, 1973, was a landmark event not just in sports history but also in the broader fight for gender equality. This historic match transcended the realm of tennis, symbolizing a major step forward in the movement for women's rights and equality.

Context and Background:

1. The Gender Dynamics of the Time:

o Societal Views: In the early 1970s, gender roles and expectations were rigid, with women's sports often receiving less recognition and support compared to men's sports. There were prevalent stereotypes about women's athletic abilities and their place in the competitive world.

o The Push for Equality: The women's liberation movement was gaining momentum, advocating for equal rights and opportunities in various aspects of society, including sports.

2. Bobby Riggs' Challenge:

o Riggs' Background: Bobby Riggs, a former World No. 1 male tennis player and a self-proclaimed tennis hustler, had retired from professional tennis but remained active in the sport through exhibition matches. He was known for his flamboyant personality and trash-talking.

o The Challenge: Riggs, who was 55 years old at the time, claimed that he could still beat any of the top female players, asserting that even the best women's players were inferior to male players. He challenged Billie Jean King, a leading figure in women's tennis and an advocate for gender equality, to a match.

The Match:
1. Event Details:

o Date and Venue: The match took place on September 20, 1973, at the Houston Astrodome in Houston, Texas.

o Match Setup: The match was played as a best-of-three sets exhibition, and it was highly publicized as a battle not only between two players but also as a symbolic contest between the sexes.

2. Billie Jean King's Performance:

o Gameplay: King approached the match with a strategic mindset and focus. She demonstrated her superior skills, athleticism, and composure throughout the match.

o Victory: King won decisively with a score of 6-4, 6-3. Her performance was a testament to her preparation and skill, and she handled the match with grace and confidence.

Impact and Significance:
1. Advancement of Gender Equality:

o Breaking Stereotypes: King's victory was a powerful statement that challenged existing gender stereotypes and demonstrated that women could compete at the highest levels of professional sports. It was a significant moment in the fight for gender equality.

○ Public Perception: The match drew a large television audience and media coverage, bringing widespread attention to issues of gender inequality in sports. King's win was seen as a victory for women and a step towards greater recognition and respect for female athletes.

2. Billie Jean King's Legacy:

○ Champion for Equality: Billie Jean King became an iconic figure not just for her tennis achievements but also for her advocacy for women's rights and gender equality. Her victory in the "Battle of the Sexes" solidified her role as a trailblazer in both sports and social justice.

○ Ongoing Influence: King's efforts contributed to the establishment of more equitable opportunities and recognition for female athletes. Her legacy continues to inspire new generations of athletes and advocates for gender equality.

3. Cultural Impact:

○ Symbol of Change: The "Battle of the Sexes" became a symbol of the broader social changes of the 1970s. It highlighted the growing movement for gender equality and the breaking down of traditional barriers and prejudices.

○ Inspiration: King's victory served as an inspiration for women and girls pursuing careers in sports and other fields traditionally dominated by men. It emphasized the importance of challenging stereotypes and advocating for equal opportunities.

Conclusion:

Billie Jean King's triumph over Bobby Riggs in the 1973 "Battle of the Sexes" was a historic event that transcended the sport of tennis. It symbolized a significant moment in the fight for gender equality, challenging existing stereotypes and advancing the cause of women's rights. King's performance and victory were not only a testament to her extraordinary talent but also a powerful statement on the progress towards equality and the potential for women to achieve greatness in all areas of life. The match remains a landmark event that continues to resonate in discussions about gender, sports, and social change.

Billie Jean King's Impact After the "Battle of the Sexes"

Billie Jean King's victory over Bobby Riggs in the 1973 "Battle of the Sexes" was a defining moment in both sports history and the broader fight for gender equality. Beyond the immediate fame and attention the match garnered, King's impact has been profound and multifaceted. Here's a look at the significant ways in which King influenced the world after this iconic match:

1. Advancement of Women's Sports:

● Increased Visibility: King's victory brought substantial visibility to women's sports, helping to elevate the profile of female athletes and encourage media coverage. Her success was instrumental in demonstrating that women's sports could attract significant attention and generate substantial interest.

● Professional Opportunities: King's advocacy for women's sports contributed to the creation of professional opportunities for female athletes. She was a key figure in the establishment of the Women's Tennis Association (WTA) in 1973, which provided a platform for female players to compete on more equitable terms with their male counterparts.

2. Title IX and Gender Equity:

• Support for Title IX: Billie Jean King was a vocal supporter of Title IX, the landmark U.S. legislation passed in 1972 that prohibits discrimination based on sex in federally funded education programs and activities. Her advocacy played a crucial role in promoting the importance of this legislation, which significantly increased opportunities for women in sports and education.

• Educational and Athletic Growth: Title IX's implementation led to greater investment in women's sports at educational institutions, contributing to the growth and development of women's athletic programs across the United States. King's efforts helped highlight the importance of these changes and the need for continued progress toward gender equity.

3. Advocacy for LGBTQ+ Rights:

• Publicly Coming Out: In 1981, King publicly came out as gay during a period when LGBTQ+ issues were less openly discussed. Her decision to share her sexuality was groundbreaking and contributed to increasing visibility and acceptance for LGBTQ+ individuals in sports and beyond.

• Support for LGBTQ+ Rights: King has been an advocate for LGBTQ+ rights throughout her life, using her platform to promote acceptance and equality. Her activism has helped pave the way for greater inclusion and understanding within the sports community and society at large.

4. Philanthropy and Social Impact:

• Billie Jean King Leadership Initiative: In 2014, King established the Billie Jean King Leadership Initiative, which focuses on advancing women and minorities in leadership positions, promoting diversity and inclusion in the workplace, and addressing social justice issues. The initiative continues her legacy of advocacy and support for equitable opportunities.

• Public Speaking and Education: King has continued to use her voice to speak on issues of gender equality, diversity, and social justice. Her speeches, writings, and public appearances have contributed to ongoing conversations about equity and have inspired many to engage in these important issues.

5. Influence on Future Generations:

• Inspiration to Athletes: King's achievements and advocacy have inspired countless female athletes to pursue their dreams and challenge societal expectations. Her success has served as a powerful example of what can be accomplished through perseverance and commitment.

• Mentorship and Support: King has mentored and supported young athletes, especially women, helping to guide and empower them in their athletic careers and beyond. Her influence extends to those who have followed in her footsteps, continuing to impact the world of sports.

Conclusion:

Billie Jean King's impact following the "Battle of the Sexes" has been far-reaching and enduring. Her contributions to women's sports, advocacy for gender and LGBTQ+ equality, philanthropic efforts, and influence on future generations reflect her commitment to creating a more equitable and inclusive society. King's legacy extends beyond her athletic achievements to encompass her role as a trailblazer and advocate for social change, making her a pivotal figure in both sports and social justice.

Roger Federer's 20th Grand Slam Title (2018)

The Achievement:

Roger Federer's 20th Grand Slam title, secured at the Australian Open on January 28, 2018, was a landmark achievement in men's tennis. This victory not only added to Federer's already illustrious career but also cemented his status as one of the greatest tennis players of all time.

Context and Background:

1. Federer's Career:

○ Early Success: Roger Federer, known for his graceful play and technical excellence, had already established himself as a dominant force in tennis by the time of his 20th Grand Slam win. His career began to flourish in the early 2000s, and he quickly became known for his versatile game and sportsmanship.

○ Previous Grand Slam Titles: By 2018, Federer had won 19 Grand Slam titles, tied with Rafael Nadal and Novak Djokovic for the most in the Open Era. The competition among these three players had been intense, with each breaking records and setting new benchmarks in the sport.

2. 2018 Australian Open:

○ Tournament Significance: The Australian Open, held annually in Melbourne, is one of the four Grand Slam tournaments and is known for its challenging conditions and high level of competition.

○ Federer's Performance: Federer entered the 2018 Australian Open as the defending champion. His performance throughout the tournament was impressive, showcasing his skill, resilience, and ability to perform under pressure.

The 20th Grand Slam Victory:
1. The Final Match:

○ Opponent: Federer faced Marin Čilić, a Croatian player known for his powerful game and previous Grand Slam success. The final was held on January 28, 2018.

○ Match Details: Federer won the match in five sets with scores of 6-2, 6-7(5), 6-3, 3-6, 6-1. Despite facing a tough opponent and a grueling five-set battle, Federer demonstrated remarkable endurance and tactical acumen.

2. Significance of the Win:

○ Career Milestone: Securing his 20th Grand Slam title was a significant milestone for Federer. It marked a new record in men's tennis, surpassing the previous achievements of other great players and highlighting his longevity and consistency at the highest level of the sport.

○ Emotional Moment: Federer's victory was deeply emotional for both him and his fans. It was a testament to his enduring passion for the game and his ability to perform at an elite level even as he approached his late 30s.

Impact and Significance:
1. Legacy and Records:

○ Tennis Legacy: Federer's 20th Grand Slam title added to his already impressive legacy. His career achievements include numerous records in both Grand Slam victories and ATP titles. The win further solidified his reputation as one of the greatest tennis players in history.

○ Influence on the Sport: Federer's success has influenced the next generation of players and has set a high standard for excellence in tennis. His approach to the game, sportsmanship, and professionalism serve as a model for aspiring players.

2. Fan and Cultural Impact:

○ Global Recognition: Federer's victory was celebrated by tennis fans around the world and received extensive media coverage. It was a moment of joy and pride for his supporters and for tennis enthusiasts who admired his career.

○ Enduring Popularity: Federer's impact extends beyond his on-court achievements. His charm, elegance, and philanthropy have endeared him to fans and have made him a global ambassador for the sport.

3. Future Implications:

○ Ongoing Rivalries: Federer's 20th Grand Slam win continued to fuel the ongoing rivalry between him, Rafael Nadal, and Novak Djokovic. Each player has competed fiercely for Grand Slam titles, contributing to one of the most exciting eras in tennis history.

○ Inspirational Figure: Federer's achievement at the Australian Open serves as an inspiration to athletes of all ages. It demonstrates that with dedication, perseverance, and passion, extraordinary accomplishments can be achieved even in the later stages of a career.

Conclusion:

Roger Federer's 20th Grand Slam title at the 2018 Australian Open was a career-defining moment in men's tennis. It highlighted his exceptional talent, resilience, and dedication to the sport. The victory not only added to his impressive list of achievements but also reinforced his status as one of the greatest players in tennis history. Federer's legacy extends beyond his titles; it encompasses his influence on the sport, his contributions to tennis culture, and high role as an inspiration to players and fans around the world.

Serena Williams' 23rd Grand Slam Title (2017)

The Achievement:

Serena Williams' 23rd Grand Slam title, achieved at the 2017 Australian Open, was a landmark moment in women's tennis and in sports history. Her victory not only solidified her place as one of the greatest female athletes of all time but also broke records and challenged norms in the world of sports.

Context and Background:

1. Williams' Career:

o Early Success: Serena Williams, alongside her sister Venus, emerged as a dominant force in tennis in the late 1990s and early 2000s. Known for her powerful serve, athleticism, and mental toughness, Serena quickly rose through the ranks of professional tennis.

o Previous Grand Slam Titles: By the time of her 23rd title, Serena had already established herself as a dominant player, with multiple Grand Slam victories and numerous records to her name. Her pursuit of Grand Slam titles was not just about personal achievement but also about setting new benchmarks in women's tennis.

2. 2017 Australian Open:

o Tournament Significance: The Australian Open, held in Melbourne, is one of the four Grand Slam tournaments and is renowned for its challenging conditions and high level of competition. Serena entered the 2017 tournament as the defending champion.

o Williams' Performance: Serena Williams' performance throughout the 2017 Australian Open was exceptional. She demonstrated her remarkable skill, endurance, and resilience, overcoming tough opponents to secure the title.

The 23rd Grand Slam Victory:
1. The Final Match:

o Opponent: In the final, Serena faced her older sister, Venus Williams, in a historic all-Williams final. Venus, a formidable player in her own right, had also achieved significant success in her career.

o Match Details: Serena won the match with a score of 6-4, 6-4. The victory was a testament to her ability to perform at the highest level under pressure, even against a close family member and rival.

2. Significance of the Win:

o Record-Breaking Achievement: Serena Williams' 23rd Grand Slam title surpassed the previous record of 22 Grand Slam titles held by Steffi Graf, setting a new benchmark in women's tennis. This achievement underscored Serena's dominance and longevity in the sport.

o Historical Context: Serena's victory was also significant in the context of the Open Era, where the greatest players compete for Grand Slam titles. Her 23rd title positioned her as one of the most accomplished players in tennis history.

Impact and Significance:

1. Breaking Records:

o Grand Slam Record: Serena's 23rd Grand Slam title broke Steffi Graf's record for the most Grand Slam singles titles in the Open Era. This achievement highlighted Serena's exceptional career and her ability to maintain a high level of performance over an extended period.

o Cultural Impact: The record-breaking win drew widespread attention and admiration, contributing to Serena's status as a trailblazer in women's sports. Her achievements challenged existing norms and perceptions about female athletes.

2. Challenging Norms:

o Gender and Racial Barriers: Serena Williams' success has been a powerful statement against gender and racial barriers in sports. As an African American woman in a predominantly white sport, Serena has faced and overcome numerous challenges, using her platform to advocate for equality and representation.

o Inspiration for Future Generations: Serena's achievements have inspired countless young athletes, particularly women and people of color, to pursue their dreams and challenge societal expectations. Her success serves as a powerful example of overcoming obstacles and achieving greatness.

3. Legacy and Influence:

o Impact on Women's Sports: Serena Williams' career has had a profound impact on women's sports, increasing visibility and respect for female athletes. Her achievements have contributed to greater investment and interest in women's tennis and sports in general.

○ Ongoing Influence: Serena's influence extends beyond her athletic accomplishments. She is also known for her advocacy on social issues, including gender equality, racial justice, and health. Her legacy is characterized by both her sporting excellence and her commitment to making a positive difference in the world.

Conclusion:

Serena Williams' 23rd Grand Slam title at the 2017 Australian Open was a historic achievement that highlighted her exceptional talent, determination, and resilience. The victory not only broke records but also challenged norms and set new standards in women's sports. Serena's impact extends beyond her on-court success; she has become a symbol of excellence, empowerment, and advocacy, inspiring future generations and making a significant contribution to the world of sports and beyond.

Chapter 8: Triumphs in the Face of Adversity

<u>Jim Abbott's No-Hitter (1993)</u>

The Achievement:

Jim Abbott's no-hitter on September 4, 1993, while pitching for the New York Yankees against the Cleveland Indians, is one of the most inspiring and remarkable moments in baseball history. Abbott, who was born without a right hand, accomplished the feat against the odds, showcasing his exceptional skill and determination.

Context and Background:

1. Jim Abbott's Career:

o Early Life and Challenges: Jim Abbott was born on September 19, 1967, with a condition known as congenital limb reduction, which left him without a right hand. Despite this challenge, Abbott excelled in baseball from a young age, using his left hand to pitch and field with remarkable effectiveness.

o Collegiate Success: Abbott played college baseball for the University of Michigan, where he gained national attention for his exceptional pitching. His success in college led to a highly anticipated professional career.

2. Professional Journey:

o MLB Debut: Abbott made his Major League Baseball (MLB) debut with the California Angels in 1989. His unique pitching style and perseverance quickly garnered respect from teammates, opponents, and fans.

○ Achievements: In addition to his no-hitter, Abbott had a successful MLB career, including pitching a complete game for the Chicago White Sox in 1993. He was known for his strong work ethic, competitive spirit, and skillful pitching.

The No-Hitter:
1. The Game:

○ Date and Opponent: On September 4, 1993, Jim Abbott pitched a no-hitter for the New York Yankees against the Cleveland Indians at Yankee Stadium. The game was a significant moment not only in Abbott's career but in MLB history.

○ Performance Details: Abbott's performance was exceptional, as he faced 27 batters and allowed no hits, walking just three and striking out eight. His ability to pitch a no-hitter despite his physical challenge was a testament to his skill and determination.

2. Significance of the No-Hitter:

○ Overcoming Adversity: Abbott's no-hitter was particularly remarkable given his physical condition. The feat demonstrated that he could compete at the highest level of the sport and achieve something that many thought impossible.

○ Inspiration to Others: The no-hitter served as an inspiration to athletes and individuals facing their own challenges. Abbott's success highlighted the potential for overcoming obstacles through perseverance and hard work.

Impact and Significance:
1. Legacy in Baseball:

○ Historical Achievement: Jim Abbott's no-hitter remains one of the most memorable achievements in baseball history. It is celebrated as a testament to his talent and resilience, and it continues to be a source of pride and inspiration for fans and players alike.

○ Respect from Peers: Abbott's accomplishment earned him widespread respect from fellow players and coaches. His story became a symbol of how determination and skill can defy expectations and break barriers in sports.

2. Cultural and Inspirational Impact:

○ Role Model: Abbott's success has made him a role model for athletes with disabilities and those facing other personal challenges. His story demonstrates that with dedication and perseverance, one can achieve extraordinary feats regardless of physical limitations.

○ Public Recognition: Abbott's no-hitter has been featured in various media and sports discussions, highlighting his remarkable achievement and the broader message of overcoming adversity. It has also been used to inspire and motivate individuals in various fields beyond sports.

3. Post-Retirement Contributions:

○ Advocacy and Outreach: After retiring from professional baseball, Jim Abbott has been involved in various philanthropic activities and outreach programs. He has spoken at schools, conferences, and events, sharing his story and encouraging others to pursue their dreams.

○ Author and Speaker: Abbott has written books and given motivational speeches, using his experiences to inspire others and advocate for overcoming challenges and achieving personal goals.

Conclusion:

Jim Abbott's no-hitter on September 4, 1993, is a landmark achievement in baseball that goes beyond the sport itself. It represents the triumph of skill, perseverance, and determination in the face of significant physical challenges. Abbott's accomplishment remains an enduring symbol of overcoming adversity and serves as an inspiration to athletes and individuals everywhere. His legacy is defined not only by his remarkable performance on the mound but also by his continued efforts to inspire and support others in their personal and professional journeys.

Kerri Strug's Vault (1996)

The Achievement:

Kerri Strug's vault at the 1996 Summer Olympics in Atlanta is one of the most dramatic and inspiring moments in Olympic history. Strug, a member of the U.S. women's gymnastics team known as the "Magnificent Seven," performed a crucial vault on an injured ankle that helped secure the team's first-ever Olympic gold medal in gymnastics.

Context and Background:

1. The 1996 Olympics:

○ Team Dynamics: The U.S. women's gymnastics team, including Kerri Strug, was competing in the team all-around competition. The team was favored to win a medal, but they faced strong competition from other countries, notably Russia.

○ Team Performance: Leading up to the final rotation, the U.S. team was in a tight contest with the Russian team. The outcome of the competition hinged on the final rotation, where the vault was the last event.

2. Kerri Strug's Career:

○ Early Achievements: Kerri Strug, born on November 19, 1977, had already established herself as a talented gymnast with a series of national and international accolades. Her performances had made her a key member of the U.S. team.

○ Injury and Challenges: Strug was dealing with an ankle injury leading up to the Olympics. Despite the pain and challenges, she was determined to contribute to her team's success.

The Vault:
1. The Situation:

○ Final Rotation: As the team reached the vault, the pressure was immense. The U.S. needed strong performances to clinch the gold medal, and Strug's performance was critical.

○ Strug's Injury: Strug had injured her ankle during her first vault attempt. Despite the pain, she made the decision to compete on the second attempt, knowing how crucial it was for her team's success.

2. The Performance:

○ Second Vault: On July 23, 1996, Kerri Strug executed a memorable vault despite her injury. She landed with a dramatic and painful landing but performed well enough to secure a high score for her team.

○ Impact on the Score: Strug's vault helped the U.S. team secure the gold medal by a narrow margin. Her performance was a critical factor in the team's victory over Russia.

Impact and Significance:
1. Immediate Reaction:

○ National Celebration: Strug's vault was celebrated as a symbol of courage and determination. Her performance was widely covered in the media and was met with immense admiration from fans and fellow athletes.

○ Historic Achievement: The gold medal was a historic achievement for U.S. women's gymnastics, marking the first time the U.S. team won gold in the team competition.

2. Legacy and Inspiration:

○ Symbol of Perseverance: Kerri Strug's vault became a symbol of perseverance and dedication. Her willingness to compete despite her injury and her crucial contribution to the team's success inspired many.

o Influence on Gymnastics: Strug's performance brought attention to the sport and inspired a new generation of gymnasts. Her courage and commitment to her team have been cited as exemplary traits for athletes in all sports.

3. Post-Olympics:

o Recognition and Honors: Kerri Strug received numerous accolades and honors following the Olympics, including the U.S. Olympic Committee's Sportswoman of the Year award. Her story continues to be a source of inspiration in the sports community.

o Advocacy and Public Appearances: Strug has used her platform to speak about her experiences, advocate for the sport, and participate in various charitable activities. Her story is often highlighted in discussions about Olympic heroism and athletic dedication.

Conclusion:

Kerri Strug's vault at the 1996 Summer Olympics is an enduring symbol of courage, determination, and team spirit. Her performance on an injured ankle to secure the U.S. women's gymnastics team's first gold medal remains one of the most memorable moments in Olympic history. Strug's legacy is defined not only by her athletic achievement but also by her inspiring demonstration of perseverance and dedication. Her story continues to resonate with athletes and fans, serving as a powerful example of overcoming adversity and achieving greatness in the face of challenges.

Greg Louganis' Perfect Dive After Hitting His Head (1988)

The Achievement:

Greg Louganis' performance in the 1988 Seoul Olympics, particularly his perfect dive after hitting his head on the diving board, is a dramatic and inspirational moment in Olympic history. Louganis, already a dominant figure in diving, showcased not only his incredible skill but also his resilience and determination in overcoming a serious injury to win gold.

Context and Background:

1. Greg Louganis' Career:

○ Early Success: Greg Louganis, born on January 29, 1960, is considered one of the greatest divers of all time. By the time of the 1988 Seoul Olympics, Louganis had already achieved significant success, including winning gold medals at the 1984 Los Angeles Olympics.

○ Preparation and Pressure: Heading into the 1988 Olympics, Louganis was the defending champion and a favorite to win gold. His reputation was built on his technical precision and artistry in diving.

2. The 1988 Seoul Olympics:

○ Competition Context: The diving competition was highly competitive, with many strong divers vying for medals. Louganis was aiming to defend his titles from the previous Olympics and cement his legacy in the sport.

The Incident:
1. Preliminary Round Mishap:

o Accident: On April 19, 1988, during the preliminary rounds of the men's platform diving event, Greg Louganis hit his head on the diving board while executing a dive. The impact caused a visible cut on his forehead, and there was concern about whether he could continue.

o Immediate Reaction: Despite the injury, Louganis exhibited remarkable composure and resilience. He was checked by medical personnel and, after receiving treatment, was determined to continue competing.

2. The Perfect Dive:

o Final Performance: After the accident, Louganis returned to the platform for his final dives. In a dramatic display of skill and mental fortitude, he delivered a perfect dive, receiving a 10 from all judges for his final performance.

o Score and Outcome: Louganis' perfect dive helped him secure the gold medal in the 10-meter platform event. His performance was celebrated for its technical excellence and the remarkable ability to overcome a significant setback.

Impact and Significance:
1. Immediate Recognition:

o Historic Moment: Louganis' ability to deliver a flawless dive despite the injury was met with widespread acclaim. His performance was hailed as one of the greatest moments in Olympic diving history.

o Media Coverage: The incident and his subsequent gold medal win received extensive media coverage, highlighting

Louganis' courage and skill. His story was a focal point of Olympic coverage and public discussion.

2. Legacy and Influence:

○ Inspiration to Athletes: Louganis' performance served as an inspiration to athletes across various sports. His ability to overcome adversity and deliver under pressure is often cited as a model of mental toughness and resilience.

○ Impact on Diving: Louganis' achievements and his dramatic moment in Seoul contributed to the elevated profile of diving. His technical skills and performances helped popularize the sport and set new standards for future divers.

3. Post-Olympics:

○ Advocacy and Personal Life: After retiring from competitive diving, Louganis became an advocate for various causes, including HIV/AIDS awareness. He publicly revealed his HIV-positive status and worked to reduce stigma and promote understanding.

○ Public Recognition: Louganis has received numerous awards and honors for his contributions to diving and his advocacy work. He remains a respected figure in the sports community and beyond.

Conclusion:

Greg Louganis' perfect dive at the 1988 Seoul Olympics, following his head injury, stands as one of the most compelling moments in Olympic history. His extraordinary performance under challenging conditions exemplifies the spirit of perseverance and excellence in sports. Louganis' legacy extends beyond his diving achievements, encompassing his impact as an advocate and role model. His story continues to inspire athletes and individuals, demonstrating the power of resilience and determination in overcoming obstacles and achieving greatness.

Chapter 9: Legendary Moments in Baseball

Boston Red Sox Break the Curse (2004)

The Achievement:

The Boston Red Sox breaking the "Curse of the Bambino" by winning the 2004 World Series was a momentous event in baseball history. After an 86-year drought without a championship, the Red Sox's victory was celebrated as a historic and emotional triumph for the team and its fans.

Context and Background:

1. The Curse of the Bambino:

○ Origin of the Curse: The "Curse of the Bambino" originated from the trade of Babe Ruth, also known as the Bambino, from the Boston Red Sox to the New York Yankees in 1919. Ruth's departure marked the beginning of a long period of disappointment for the Red Sox, who struggled to win the World Series despite having strong teams.

○ Historical Frustrations: Over the years, the Red Sox experienced numerous near-misses and heartbreaking losses, which were popularly attributed to the curse. The team's inability to secure a championship became a defining aspect of their identity.

2. 2004 Season Overview:

o Regular Season: The 2004 Red Sox were a strong team, finishing the regular season with a record of 98-64, clinching the American League (AL) East title. They were led by a roster featuring stars like David Ortiz, Manny Ramirez, and Pedro Martínez.

o Postseason Struggles: Despite a successful regular season, the Red Sox faced a tough postseason, including a dramatic American League Championship Series (ALCS) against the New York Yankees.

The ALCS and World Series:
1. The ALCS Comeback:

o Historic Deficit: The Red Sox were down 3-0 in the ALCS against the Yankees, facing elimination. The series appeared to be a repeat of past disappointments, but the Red Sox mounted an unprecedented comeback.

o The "Greatest Comeback": The Red Sox won the next four games, completing the first-ever comeback from a 3-0 deficit in a best-of-seven series. Key moments included a game-winning hit by David Ortiz and an incredible pitching performance by Curt Schilling, despite an injury that led to his "bloody sock" appearance.

2. The World Series Victory:

o The Series Against the St. Louis Cardinals: The Red Sox faced the St. Louis Cardinals in the World Series, which began on October 23, 2004. The Red Sox dominated the series, winning in a four-game sweep.

○ Final Game and Celebration: The Red Sox clinched the World Series title with a 3-0 victory in Game 4, concluding the series on October 27, 2004. The win was met with jubilation from fans who had long awaited this moment.

Impact and Significance:
1. Ending the Curse:

○ Emotional Release: The Red Sox's victory was a profound emotional release for the team and its fans. The end of the "Curse of the Bambino" was seen as a symbolic overcoming of decades of frustration and disappointment.

○ Historical Context: The 2004 championship was celebrated not just as a victory, but as the end of an era of historical anguish for the Red Sox and their supporters.

2. Cultural Impact:

○ Fan Celebrations: The Red Sox's win led to widespread celebrations across Boston and among Red Sox fans worldwide. The championship parade in Boston drew hundreds of thousands of fans, marking a joyous occasion for the city.

○ Media and Popular Culture: The 2004 World Series and the Red Sox's comeback became a prominent story in sports media and popular culture. The narrative of breaking the curse was widely covered and discussed.

3. Team Legacy and Influence:

○ Team's Success: The 2004 championship was a significant achievement that paved the way for continued success. The

Red Sox went on to win additional World Series titles in 2007, 2013, and 2018.

○ Impact on Fans and Baseball: The 2004 victory solidified the Red Sox's place in baseball lore and served as an inspirational story of overcoming adversity. It also reshaped the team's identity and history, marking a new era of success.

Conclusion:

The Boston Red Sox breaking the "Curse of the Bambino" by winning the 2004 World Series is a landmark moment in sports history. The achievement not only ended an 86-year championship drought but also provided a dramatic and emotional climax to a long-standing narrative of frustration. The victory is celebrated as a symbol of perseverance, redemption, and the enduring passion of baseball fans. The Red Sox's triumph in 2004 remains a defining moment in the team's history and a source of inspiration for sports enthusiasts everywhere.

Bobby Thomson's "Shot Heard 'Round the World" (1951)

The Dramatic Home Run:

On October 3, 1951, in the final game of the National League (NL) pennant race between the New York Giants and the Brooklyn Dodgers, Bobby Thomson hit one of the most iconic home runs in baseball history. Known as the "Shot Heard 'Round the World," Thomson's dramatic three-run homer in the bottom of the ninth inning not only clinched the pennant for the Giants but also became one of the most memorable moments in sports history.

The game, played at the Polo Grounds in New York, was a crucial contest, as the Giants and Dodgers had finished the regular season tied for first place. The tension was palpable as the teams battled for the chance to advance to the World Series. With the Giants trailing 4-1 entering the bottom of the ninth, Thomson's home run, which came on a pitch thrown by the Dodgers' Ralph Branca, turned the game around. The ball sailed into the left-field stands, giving the Giants a 5-4 victory and securing the NL pennant.

Its Place in Baseball Lore:

Bobby Thomson's "Shot Heard 'Round the World" holds a special place in baseball lore for several reasons:

1. Historical Significance: The game and the home run occurred during one of the most intense and dramatic pennant races in baseball history. The Giants' comeback from a 13-game deficit in mid-August to force a tie with the Dodgers was remarkable, and Thomson's home run epitomized the climax of this thrilling season.

2. Impact on the Game: Thomson's home run not only determined the NL champion but also became a symbol of the drama and excitement inherent in baseball. It is often

cited as one of the greatest moments in sports history, demonstrating the capacity of the game to produce unforgettable, high-stakes moments.

3. Cultural Impact: The phrase "Shot Heard 'Round the World" has transcended baseball, becoming a metaphor for moments of extraordinary impact and significance. It draws parallels with historical events and moments of global importance, reflecting the profound effect of Thomson's home run on the baseball community and beyond.

4. Enduring Legacy: The home run has been immortalized in numerous ways, including in books, documentaries, and broadcasts. The moment is a staple of baseball highlight reels and has been celebrated in various forms of media, preserving its place in the sport's rich history.

5. Emotional Resonance: The dramatic nature of the home run, coming at the end of a season filled with tension and excitement, adds to its legendary status. Thomson's hit is remembered not only for its impact on the game but also for the emotional response it elicited from players and fans alike.

6. Historical Context: The event occurred during a period of significant change in baseball, as the sport was transitioning into a new era with increased media coverage and fan engagement. The "Shot Heard 'Round the World" captured the imagination of a generation of baseball fans and became a defining moment of that era.

Conclusion:

Bobby Thomson's "Shot Heard 'Round the World" is more than just a historic home run; it is a quintessential moment in baseball history that captures the drama, excitement, and emotional highs of the sport. The home run's lasting impact on baseball lore and its place in the cultural imagination underscore its significance as one of the greatest moments in sports history. The dramatic nature of Thomson's hit, combined with the context of the 1951 pennant race, ensures that the "Shot Heard 'Round the World" will be remembered as a defining and iconic moment in the annals of baseball.

Bo Jackson's All-Star Home Run (1989)

The Achievement:

Bo Jackson's home run during the 1989 MLB All-Star Game is a defining moment in the career of one of the most remarkable dual-sport athletes in history. Jackson's homer not only showcased his prodigious power and athleticism but also solidified his legacy as a versatile and extraordinary sports figure.

Context and Background:

1. Bo Jackson's Career:

○ Multi-Sport Excellence: Bo Jackson, born on November 30, 1962, is renowned for his achievements in both Major League Baseball (MLB) and the National Football League (NFL). Jackson played for the Kansas City Royals in baseball and the Los Angeles Raiders in football, earning acclaim in both sports.

○ All-Star Status: By 1989, Jackson was a prominent MLB player known for his powerful hitting and impressive outfield play. He had established himself as one of the most exciting and dynamic players in baseball.

2. The 1989 MLB All-Star Game:

○ Game Context: The 1989 MLB All-Star Game was held on July 11 at the Seattle Kingdome in Seattle, Washington. The game featured the best players from the American League (AL) and the National League (NL), providing a stage for baseball's top talent.

○ Jackson's Selection: Bo Jackson was selected as an All-Star, representing the American League. His inclusion in the All-Star Game was a testament to his outstanding performance during the regular season.

The Home Run:

1. The Moment:

○ Home Run Details: In the top of the 4th inning, Bo Jackson stepped up to the plate against National League pitcher Rick Reuschel. With one out and a runner on first base, Jackson hit a majestic home run over the center field fence, demonstrating his tremendous power and athleticism.

○ Spectacular Display: The home run was notable for its impressive distance and the dramatic way it showcased Jackson's raw power. His swing and follow-through highlighted his exceptional athletic ability.

2. Impact and Reaction:

○ Audience Reaction: The crowd at the Kingdome erupted in excitement as Jackson's home run sailed out of the park. The moment was celebrated by fans and commentators as a remarkable display of athletic prowess.

○ Media Coverage: The home run was widely covered in the media and became a memorable highlight of the 1989 All-Star Game. It reinforced Jackson's reputation as a remarkable and multi-talented athlete.

Impact and Significance:

1. Bo Jackson's Legacy:

○ Dual-Sport Fame: Jackson's All-Star home run added to his legacy as one of the most remarkable dual-sport athletes in history. His ability to excel in both baseball and football set him apart from his peers and contributed to his iconic status.

○ Athletic Prowess: The home run demonstrated Jackson's extraordinary physical abilities and contributed to the perception of him as one of the greatest athletes of his era. His power and skill on the field were highlighted by this memorable moment.

2. Cultural and Popular Impact:

○ Iconic Moment: Jackson's home run became one of the defining moments of his baseball career and is often cited as a key highlight of the 1989 All-Star Game. The moment has been celebrated in various sports media and retrospectives.

○ Inspiration: Jackson's achievement continues to inspire athletes and sports enthusiasts, symbolizing the potential for greatness in multiple sports and the impact of exceptional athletic talent.

3. Influence on Baseball and Football:

○ Legacy in Baseball: Jackson's performance in the 1989 All-Star Game remains a significant highlight of his baseball career. His ability to deliver in high-pressure situations reinforced his reputation as a clutch performer.

○ Impact on Sports Culture: Jackson's dual-sport career and memorable moments like his All-Star home run contributed to a broader appreciation of multi-talented athletes and the excitement they bring to sports.

Conclusion:

Bo Jackson's home run during the 1989 MLB All-Star Game is a defining moment in the career of one of sports' greatest athletes. The home run showcased Jackson's exceptional power and athleticism, solidifying his legacy as a remarkable dual-sport star. The moment remains a celebrated highlight in sports history, symbolizing Jackson's impact on baseball and football and his extraordinary athletic abilities. His All-Star home run continues to be remembered as a testament to his greatness and versatility in the world of sports.

Chapter 10: Modern Marvels

Michael Phelps' 8 Gold Medals (2008)

The Achievement:

Michael Phelps' historic performance at the 2008 Beijing Olympics, where he won eight gold medals, is considered one of the most extraordinary achievements in the history of the Olympic Games. Phelps' dominance in swimming set a new standard for excellence in the sport and elevated his status as one of the greatest athletes of all time.

Context and Background:

1. Michael Phelps' Career:

o Early Success: Born on June 30, 1985, Michael Phelps began his swimming career at a young age, showing remarkable talent and potential. By the 2004 Athens Olympics, Phelps had already made a significant mark, winning six gold medals and two bronze medals.

o 2008 Beijing Olympics: Heading into the 2008 Beijing Olympics, Phelps was the defending Olympic champion in multiple events and was widely anticipated to be a major contender for gold medals.

2. The Beijing Olympics:

o Competition Overview: The 2008 Olympics took place from August 8 to August 24 in Beijing, China. The swimming events were held at the Water Cube, a state-of-the-art aquatic center that provided a spectacular venue for the competition.

○ Phelps' Events: Phelps competed in a total of eight events, including the 100m and 200m freestyle, 200m and 400m individual medley, 50m freestyle, 100m butterfly, 200m butterfly, and the 4x100m and 4x400m medley relays.

The Performance:

1. Event Wins and Records:

○ Gold Medal Victories: Michael Phelps won gold medals in all eight of his events, an unprecedented achievement. His victories included:

- 100m Freestyle: 47.51 seconds

- 200m Freestyle: 1:42.96

- 400m Freestyle: 3:08.24

- 100m Butterfly: 50.58 seconds

- 200m Butterfly: 1:52.03

- 200m Individual Medley: 1:54.23

- 400m Individual Medley: 4:03.84

- 4x100m Medley Relay: 3:29.34

- 4x400m Medley Relay: 6:59.03

○ World Records: In addition to winning gold, Phelps set world records in seven of the eight events he competed in. His performances were characterized by his speed, technique, and strategic excellence, further solidifying his dominance in the sport.

2. Significant Moments:

○ Close Races: Some of Phelps' victories were achieved by very narrow margins, including his dramatic win in the 100m butterfly, where he won by just 0.01 seconds. These close finishes added to the excitement and significance of his achievements.

○ Team Contributions: Phelps' performances in relay events demonstrated his ability to contribute to team success, as well as his individual prowess.

Impact and Significance:
1. Setting New Standards:

○ Olympic Record: Phelps' achievement of winning eight gold medals in a single Olympics set a new standard for excellence in swimming and the Olympics as a whole. His performance highlighted the possibility of achieving multiple gold medals in a single Games.

○ Athletic Legacy: Phelps' dominance and record-breaking performances established him as the greatest swimmer in history and contributed to a broader appreciation for the sport of swimming.

2. Cultural and Popular Impact:

○ Global Recognition: Phelps' success at the Beijing Olympics brought him international fame and recognition. He became a global sports icon, admired for his dedication, skill, and competitive spirit.

○ Inspiration: Phelps' achievements inspired countless swimmers and athletes around the world. His success demonstrated the results of hard work, dedication, and the pursuit of excellence.

3. Impact on Swimming:

○ Increased Interest: Phelps' success contributed to increased interest and viewership in swimming. The sport gained greater visibility and popularity, inspiring a new generation of swimmers and fans.

○ Advancements in Training: Phelps' achievements also influenced advancements in training and technique, as athletes and coaches sought to replicate his success and improve performance in the sport.

Conclusion:

Michael Phelps' eight gold medals at the 2008 Beijing Olympics represent one of the greatest achievements in Olympic history. His dominance in swimming, characterized by record-breaking performances and multiple gold medals, set a new standard for excellence in the sport. Phelps' success not only solidified his legacy as one of the greatest athletes of all time but also inspired a global audience and elevated the profile of swimming on the world stage. His achievements at the Beijing Olympics continue to be celebrated as a remarkable testament to athletic prowess and dedication.

Tiger Woods' First Masters Win (1997)

The Achievement:

Tiger Woods' first Masters victory in 1997 was a watershed moment in the history of golf. His dominant performance at Augusta National not only marked the beginning of an era of unparalleled success for Woods but also redefined the sport with his extraordinary talent and charisma.

Context and Background:

1. Tiger Woods' Career Up to 1997:

o Early Success: Born on December 30, 1975, Tiger Woods showed prodigious talent in golf from a young age. By the mid-1990s, he had established himself as one of the most promising young golfers with multiple amateur titles and a strong presence in college golf.

o Professional Debut: Woods turned professional in August 1996 and quickly made an impact with his remarkable skill and competitive edge. His rookie year included a few notable finishes, but his full potential was yet to be realized on the global stage.

2. The 1997 Masters Tournament:

o Tournament Overview: The Masters Tournament, held annually at Augusta National Golf Club in Augusta, Georgia, is one of golf's most prestigious events. The 1997 Masters took place from April 10 to April 13.

o Expectations and Competition: Woods entered the tournament as a young and highly touted rookie. Despite his limited professional experience, he was expected to be a strong competitor due to his impressive early career performances.

The Performance:

1. Dominant Play:

○ First Round: Woods opened the tournament with a spectacular round of 70, which placed him in a strong position. His solid play continued through the tournament, demonstrating his skill and poise under pressure.

○ Second Round: In the second round, Woods shot a 66, which included a record-setting performance on the front nine with a 30. His impressive play extended his lead and established him as the clear frontrunner.

○ Third Round: Woods' third-round score of 68 further solidified his dominance, maintaining his substantial lead over the field.

○ Final Round: In the final round, Woods shot a 69, securing a total score of 270, which was 18 under par. He won the tournament by 12 strokes, a record margin of victory at the time.

2. Historic Victory:

○ Record-Breaking Performance: Woods' victory by 12 strokes was the largest margin of victory in Masters history at that time. His performance included a series of brilliant shots and strategic play that showcased his exceptional talent.

○ Impact on Golf: Woods' win at the Masters was notable not only for the margin of victory but also for the way he redefined golf. His power, precision, and mental toughness set new standards in the sport.

Impact and Significance:
1. Redefining Golf:

o Athleticism and Skill: Woods' performance introduced a new level of athleticism and skill to the game of golf. His powerful drives, remarkable short game, and strategic approach set him apart from his peers and influenced the way golf was played and perceived.

o Increased Popularity: Woods' victory at the Masters generated widespread media attention and increased interest in golf. His success contributed to a surge in the sport's popularity, attracting new fans and inspiring a new generation of golfers.

2. Cultural Impact:

o Global Recognition: Woods' win at Augusta National elevated him to international stardom. He became one of the most recognizable and influential athletes in the world, known for his charisma, skill, and impact on the sport.

o Role Model: Woods' success provided a powerful example of what could be achieved through talent, hard work, and determination. He became a role model for aspiring golfers and athletes across various sports.

3. Legacy in Golf:

o Career Milestone: The 1997 Masters win was the first of many major victories for Woods, marking the beginning of an extraordinary career. His dominance in golf, characterized by multiple major championships and record-breaking performances, solidified his status as one of the greatest golfers of all time.

○ Influence on the Game: Woods' impact on golf extends beyond his victories. His presence led to changes in the sport's approach to fitness, training, and competition. He inspired a generation of golfers to push the boundaries of their skills and approach the game with a new level of intensity and professionalism.

Conclusion:

Tiger Woods' first Masters victory in 1997 was a landmark moment in golf history. His dominant performance redefined the sport, setting new standards for excellence and athleticism. Woods' win not only established him as a rising star but also had a profound impact on the popularity and evolution of golf. His achievements at Augusta National marked the beginning of a legendary career and left an enduring legacy in the world of sports.

Tom Brady's Seventh Super Bowl Title (2021)

The Achievement:

Tom Brady's seventh Super Bowl victory, achieved in the 2020 NFL season with the Tampa Bay Buccaneers, further cemented his legacy as the greatest quarterback in NFL history. This triumph not only added to his record-setting career but also underscored his ability to adapt and succeed in different environments.

Context and Background:

1. Tom Brady's Career Up to 2021:

○ Early Success: Tom Brady, born on August 3, 1977, began his NFL career with the New England Patriots in 2000. Over his 20 years with the Patriots, he established himself as one of the sport's most successful and iconic quarterbacks, leading the team to six Super Bowl titles.

○ Move to Tampa Bay: In March 2020, Brady signed with the Tampa Bay Buccaneers after spending two decades with New England. The move marked a significant change, as he transitioned to a new team and a new conference.

2. The 2021 Super Bowl (Super Bowl LV):

○ Tournament Overview: Super Bowl LV took place on February 7, 2021, at Raymond James Stadium in Tampa, Florida, the home stadium of the Buccaneers. The game featured the Tampa Bay Buccaneers against the Kansas City Chiefs.

○ Expectations and Competition: The Buccaneers, led by Brady, faced the defending champions, the Chiefs, led by quarterback Patrick Mahomes. The match-up was highly anticipated, with Brady aiming for his seventh title and Mahomes looking to secure his second consecutive Super Bowl win.

The Performance:
1. Dominant Play:

○ Pre-Game Preparation: Brady's leadership and experience were key factors in preparing the Buccaneers for the game. His ability to read defenses and make critical adjustments played a crucial role in the team's success.

○ Game Execution: In the Super Bowl, Brady delivered an exceptional performance. He threw for 201 yards and three touchdowns, including two to wide receiver Rob Gronkowski and one to wide receiver Antonio Brown. His precise passing and strategic play helped the Buccaneers build a commanding lead.

○ Final Outcome: The Buccaneers defeated the Chiefs 31-9. Brady was named Super Bowl MVP for his performance, marking his fifth MVP award, further solidifying his legacy.

2. Historic Victory:

○ Seventh Title: Brady's seventh Super Bowl win is the most by any player in NFL history. This victory underscored his unparalleled career achievements and set a new benchmark for excellence in professional football.

○ Impact on Legacy: Winning a Super Bowl with a new team demonstrated Brady's ability to adapt and succeed in different circumstances. It highlighted his skill, leadership, and longevity in the sport.

Impact and Significance:
1. Cementing Legacy:

○ Greatest Quarterback: Brady's seventh Super Bowl title reinforced his status as the greatest quarterback in NFL history. His career achievements, including multiple MVP awards and Super Bowl wins, distinguish him as the sport's all-time best.

○ Leadership and Adaptability: Brady's success with the Buccaneers showcased his exceptional leadership and adaptability. His ability to integrate with a new team and lead them to victory underscored his unparalleled football IQ and preparation.

2. Cultural Impact:

○ Inspiration: Brady's career and achievements serve as an inspiration to athletes across all sports. His dedication, work ethic, and ability to perform under pressure are celebrated as examples of excellence and perseverance.

○ Fan Engagement: Brady's success continues to captivate football fans and sports enthusiasts. His journey from a young quarterback with a chip on his shoulder to a seven-time Super Bowl champion resonates deeply with fans and underscores the drama and excitement of professional football.

3. Legacy in the NFL:

○ Record-Setting Career: Brady's seventh Super Bowl title contributes to a record-setting career that includes numerous records for passing yards, touchdowns, and wins. His influence on the game of football is profound and lasting.

○ Influence on the Game: Brady's career has influenced how quarterbacks are evaluated and the strategic approach to the game. His success with different teams highlights the importance of adaptability and leadership in achieving greatness.

Conclusion:

Tom Brady's seventh Super Bowl title in 2021 was a historic achievement that solidified his legacy as the greatest quarterback in NFL history. His dominant performance in Super Bowl LV, combined with his ability to excel in different environments, demonstrated his unparalleled skill and leadership. Brady's career is a testament to excellence in professional football and continues to inspire athletes and fans alike.

Chapter 11: Shocking Upsets and Unlikely Victories

<u>Buster Douglas Upsets Mike Tyson (1990)</u>

The Achievement:

Buster Douglas' victory over Mike Tyson on February 11, 1990, in Tokyo, Japan, is widely considered one of the biggest upsets in boxing history. This stunning result not only shocked the sports world but also marked a pivotal moment in heavyweight boxing.

Context and Background:

1. Mike Tyson's Dominance:

o Early Career: Mike Tyson, born June 30, 1966, became the youngest heavyweight champion in history at the age of 20 in 1986. Known for his ferocious power and aggressive style, Tyson quickly established himself as one of the most dominant fighters of his era.

o Undisputed Champion: By 1990, Tyson was the undisputed heavyweight champion and was regarded as nearly unbeatable. His reputation for knockout victories and his intimidating presence made him the most feared fighter in boxing.

2. Buster Douglas' Background:

o Career Overview: James "Buster" Douglas, born April 7, 1960, was a journeyman boxer with a solid but unremarkable career before the Tyson fight. His most notable achievements included a few regional titles, but he was not considered a top contender.

○ Pre-Fight Situation: Douglas was a 42-1 underdog heading into the fight against Tyson. Many viewed him as an unlikely challenger, and his chances of victory were seen as minimal.

The Performance:

1. Fight Preparation and Strategy:

○ Douglas' Preparation: Douglas entered the fight with a renewed focus and conditioning. He trained rigorously and was determined to prove himself against the formidable Tyson. His strategy involved utilizing his size and reach advantage, along with a disciplined approach.

○ Tyson's Readiness: Tyson, on the other hand, was dealing with personal issues and had not prepared as rigorously for the fight. His preparation was criticized for being less thorough than usual, and his focus appeared to be lacking.

2. The Fight:

○ First Half: In the early rounds, Tyson appeared to be in control, using his power to land significant punches. However, Douglas demonstrated resilience and skill, countering Tyson's attacks with effective combinations and movement.

○ Turning Point: As the fight progressed, Douglas began to assert dominance. His combination of powerful jabs, effective hooks, and strategic footwork overwhelmed Tyson, who struggled to adapt to Douglas' approach.

○ The Knockout: In the 10th round, Douglas delivered a stunning uppercut that knocked Tyson down. Tyson managed to rise, but Douglas continued his assault and ultimately knocked Tyson out with a flurry of punches, winning by knockout.

3. Historic Victory:

○ Immediate Impact: Douglas' victory over Tyson was a seismic shock in the world of boxing. It ended Tyson's reign as heavyweight champion and was considered one of the most surprising results in sports history.

○ Douglas' Title: Douglas was crowned the new heavyweight champion, and his victory was celebrated as a triumph of determination and skill against the odds.

Impact and Significance:
1. Impact on Boxing:

○ Shift in the Heavyweight Division: Douglas' win disrupted the heavyweight division's status quo, opening up new opportunities and shifting the power dynamics among heavyweight contenders. It demonstrated that even the most dominant champions could be vulnerable.

○ Tyson's Legacy: Tyson's defeat raised questions about his career and future. It marked the beginning of a period of decline for Tyson, who would face various challenges and controversies in the subsequent years.

2. Cultural Impact:

○ Inspirational Story: Douglas' victory was an inspirational story of perseverance and overcoming adversity. It resonated with fans and athletes as an example of how determination and preparation could lead to monumental success.

○ Public Reaction: The fight captured the imagination of sports fans worldwide. The shock of the upset and the dramatic nature of the fight made it a memorable moment in sports history.

3. Legacy in Boxing:

○ Douglas' Career: Despite the significance of his victory, Douglas' reign as champion was short-lived. He lost the title to Evander Holyfield later in 1990, but his win over Tyson remains a defining moment in his career.

○ Historical Context: The upset is often cited as one of the greatest moments in boxing history due to its unexpected nature and the dramatic shift it caused in the heavyweight division. It serves as a reminder of the unpredictable nature of sports.

Conclusion:

Buster Douglas' upset victory over Mike Tyson in 1990 was a historic and unprecedented moment in boxing. The fight highlighted the unpredictability of sports and the potential for extraordinary outcomes. Douglas' triumph over the seemingly invincible Tyson remains a defining moment in boxing history and continues to be celebrated for its dramatic impact and inspirational story.

<u>Ronda Rousey's 14-Second Armbar (2015)</u>

The Achievement:

Ronda Rousey's 14-second armbar submission victory over Cat Zingano at UFC 184 on February 28, 2015, is one of the most iconic and record-breaking moments in mixed martial arts (MMA) history.

This quick and decisive win further cemented Rousey's dominance in the UFC and showcased her exceptional skill and efficiency.

Context and Background:

1. Ronda Rousey's Rise:

o Early Career: Ronda Rousey, born February 1, 1987, gained prominence in MMA with her impressive judo background and a reputation for finishing fights quickly. Her transition from judo to MMA saw her become a pioneer in women's combat sports.

o UFC Championship: Rousey became the first UFC Women's Bantamweight Champion in December 2012, and her dominance in the division was characterized by a series of quick victories, largely through her signature armbar submission.

2. Cat Zingano's Background:

o Career Overview: Cat Zingano, born July 1, 1982, was a formidable opponent in the UFC women's bantamweight division. She was known for her striking and grappling skills, earning a reputation as a top contender.

o Pre-Fight Situation: Before UFC 184, Zingano had been highly regarded and was seen as a significant challenge for Rousey. She had previously won the inaugural UFC women's bantamweight title eliminator match and was considered a strong opponent.

The Performance:

1. Fight Setup:

o Anticipation and Hype: The fight between Rousey and Zingano was highly anticipated, with fans and analysts eager to see how Zingano's skills would match up against Rousey's dominance. The bout was positioned as a major event for the UFC.

o Fight Night: UFC 184 took place at the Staples Center in Los Angeles, California, and the main event featured Rousey defending her title against Zingano.

2. The Armbar Submission:

o First Round: From the outset, Rousey's intent was clear. She displayed her usual aggressive style, closing the distance and engaging Zingano with her striking.

o The Finish: Just 14 seconds into the fight, Rousey executed a flawless armbar submission. She quickly transitioned from a standing position to securing Zingano's arm, forcing her to tap out almost immediately.

o Record Achievement: The fight's quick conclusion set a new record for the fastest UFC women's bantamweight title defense, showcasing Rousey's precision and effectiveness.

Impact and Significance:
1. Impact on MMA:

o Dominance and Skill: Rousey's 14-second armbar underscored her exceptional skill and dominance in the women's bantamweight division. Her ability to finish fights rapidly set a new standard in MMA and highlighted her technical prowess.

○ Evolution of Women's MMA: Rousey's success and the quick finish further established her as a trailblazer in women's MMA. Her performances, including this record-setting victory, played a significant role in elevating the visibility and credibility of women's combat sports.

2. Cultural Impact:

○ Public Attention: The fight captured widespread media attention and reinforced Rousey's status as one of the most prominent figures in MMA. Her rapid victory added to her reputation as a dominant and charismatic athlete.

○ Inspiration for Athletes: Rousey's achievement inspired many aspiring fighters, particularly women, by demonstrating that exceptional skill and determination could lead to unprecedented success in the sport.

3. Legacy in MMA:

○ Record and Reputation: The 14-second armbar remains one of the fastest title defenses in UFC history. It is a testament to Rousey's skill and effectiveness in the Octagon.

○ Influence on Future Fighters: Rousey's performances, including this quick submission, influenced the approach and training of future fighters. Her emphasis on efficiency and technique set a benchmark for others to aspire to.

Conclusion:
Ronda Rousey's 14-second armbar submission against Cat Zingano at UFC 184 is a landmark moment in MMA history. The rapid and decisive victory showcased Rousey's extraordinary talent and solidified her position as one of the sport's greatest fighters. This

achievement not only added to her impressive legacy but also had a lasting impact on the evolution and perception of women's MMA, inspiring future generations of fighters and fans alike.

<u>The Butler Did It (2010)</u>

The Achievement:

Gordon Hayward's near-miss buzzer-beater during the 2010 NCAA Men's Basketball Championship game is one of the most memorable moments in college basketball history. His dramatic shot in the closing seconds of the game narrowly missed, and the play has since become a symbol of both the excitement and heartbreak of March Madness.

Context and Background:

1. Butler Bulldogs' Cinderella Run:

○ Team Overview: The Butler Bulldogs, led by head coach Brad Stevens, were a mid-major team from the Horizon League. Their success in the 2009-2010 season was marked by a remarkable run through the NCAA Tournament.

○ Journey to the Championship: Butler's journey to the 2010 NCAA Championship game was historic. The team, seeded fifth in the West Region, defeated higher-seeded teams, including top-seeded Syracuse and second-seeded Kansas State, to reach the Final Four and ultimately the national championship game.

2. The 2010 NCAA Championship Game:

○ Opponent: In the final, held on April 5, 2010, at Lucas Oil Stadium in Indianapolis, Butler faced the Duke Blue Devils, led by coach Mike Krzyzewski. Duke was a powerhouse program with a storied history and was considered the favorite in the matchup.

○ Game Context: The game was intensely competitive, with both teams battling hard throughout. Duke had a slim lead for most of the game, but Butler managed to stay close, setting up a dramatic conclusion.

The Performance:

1. The Final Moments:

○ Game Situation: With the game tied at 59 and just seconds remaining on the clock, Butler had the opportunity to make a final play to potentially win the game. Gordon Hayward, Butler's star player and future NBA draft pick, was given the responsibility of taking the last shot.

○ The Shot: Hayward took possession of the ball and dribbled towards the basket. With time running out, he launched a long-range shot from beyond the three-point line as the buzzer sounded. The ball sailed through the air, appearing to have a chance to win the game.

2. The Near-Miss:

○ Outcome: As the buzzer sounded, the ball hit the backboard and then the rim before bouncing out. The missed shot was a heartbreaking moment for Butler and its supporters, as the game ended with Duke emerging victorious 61-59.

○ The Impact: Hayward's shot, while unsuccessful, became iconic due to its dramatic nature and the close proximity of the miss. It represented the fine line between triumph and heartbreak in sports.

Impact and Significance:

1. Impact on College Basketball:

○ Cinderella Story: Butler's run to the championship game, highlighted by Hayward's near-miss, is remembered as one of the greatest Cinderella stories in NCAA history. The Bulldogs' journey demonstrated the excitement and unpredictability of March Madness.

○ Legacy of the Shot: The moment has become a defining highlight of the 2010 NCAA Tournament. It is frequently replayed and discussed as a symbol of both the drama of the tournament and the narrow margin between victory and defeat.

Cultural Impact:

○ Public Attention: Hayward's shot captured the imagination of fans and became a topic of widespread discussion. The image of the ball hitting the rim and bouncing out is a powerful representation of the highs and lows of sports.

○ Inspiration and Heartbreak: For many fans and players, the shot is a reminder of the emotional intensity of sports. It serves as an example of how close teams can come to achieving their dreams, even when they fall just short.

2. Legacy in Sports:

○ Butler's Reputation: The 2010 championship game solidified Butler's reputation as a respected program capable of competing at the highest level. The Bulldogs' performance continues to be a point of pride for the team and its supporters.

○ Gordon Hayward's Career: The moment also marked a significant point in Gordon Hayward's career. Hayward went on to have a successful NBA career, and his near-miss remains a notable part of his basketball journey.

Conclusion:

Gordon Hayward's near-miss buzzer-beater in the 2010 NCAA Championship game remains one of the most dramatic and memorable moments in college basketball history. The shot's close miss encapsulates the excitement and heartbreak of sports, and Butler's remarkable run to the championship is celebrated as a testament to the unpredictability and drama of March Madness. Despite the outcome, the moment is a lasting symbol of the thrilling nature of the game and the fine line between victory and defeat.

Chapter 12: Motorsport Milestones

<u>The 24 Hours of Le Mans (1966)</u>

The Achievement:

Ford's victory at the 1966 24 Hours of Le Mans is one of the most significant moments in motorsports history. It marked the culmination of Ford's intense rivalry with Ferrari, showcasing American engineering and endurance racing prowess. The race is celebrated for its dramatic conclusion and its role in reshaping the landscape of endurance racing.

Context and Background:

1. The Rivalry:

o Ford vs. Ferrari: By the mid-1960s, Ferrari was dominating endurance racing with their sleek, powerful cars. Ford, determined to prove American automotive engineering on the international stage, sought to challenge Ferrari's supremacy. This led to a heated rivalry that fueled intense competition.

o The 24 Hours of Le Mans: The 24 Hours of Le Mans is one of the most prestigious endurance races in the world, held annually in Le Mans, France. It tests the durability of both drivers and cars, requiring teams to maintain high performance over a grueling 24-hour period.

2. Ford's Strategy:

o Development of the GT40: Ford developed the GT40 specifically to compete at Le Mans. The car was designed with a focus on speed, endurance, and aerodynamics, featuring a powerful V8 engine and a sleek design.

○ Team and Drivers: Ford assembled a strong team of drivers and engineers to support their effort, including notable figures such as Carroll Shelby, who played a crucial role in developing the GT40 and leading the team's racing strategy.

The Race:
1. Pre-Race Expectations:

○ High Hopes: Ford entered the 1966 Le Mans with high expectations, having tested their GT40 extensively. Ferrari was seen as the favorite, with a strong lineup and a track record of success.

○ Initial Performance: In the early hours of the race, Ferrari's cars demonstrated their speed and reliability, while Ford's GT40s faced challenges but remained competitive.

2. The Climax:

○ Ford's Dominance: As the race progressed, Ford's GT40s gained an edge over Ferrari. The combination of speed, endurance, and strategic pit stops allowed them to take the lead.

○ Historic Finish: In a dramatic twist, the final laps of the race saw a historic moment. Ford cars finished in the top three positions, with the No. 2 GT40 driven by Bruce McLaren and Chris Amon crossing the finish line first. The race ended with a famous photo finish, where the top three Ford GT40s finished in a dramatic, closely packed finish.

Impact and Significance:
1. Breaking Ferrari's Dominance:

○ Ford's Triumph: Ford's victory at Le Mans was a significant achievement, breaking Ferrari's dominance and proving the capabilities of American engineering. It was seen as a major upset and a landmark moment in endurance racing history.

○ Cultural Impact: The victory was celebrated as a triumph of American innovation and perseverance, capturing the imagination of motorsports fans and enthusiasts around the world.

2. Legacy in Motorsports:

○ Endurance Racing: Ford's victory in 1966 helped to elevate the status of endurance racing and demonstrated the competitive nature of American teams in international events.

○ Inspiration for Future Generations: The success at Le Mans inspired future generations of racers and automotive engineers, emphasizing the importance of innovation, teamwork, and resilience in achieving success.

3. Film and Popular Culture:

○ "Ford v Ferrari": The 2019 film "Ford v Ferrari," also known as "Le Mans '66," dramatized the events of the 1966 Le Mans race and highlighted the rivalry between Ford and Ferrari. The film brought renewed attention to this historic race and celebrated the achievements of the GT40 and its drivers.

Conclusion:

Ford's historic victory at the 1966 24 Hours of Le Mans stands as one of the most celebrated moments in motorsports history. The race not only marked the end of Ferrari's dominance but also showcased the ingenuity and determination of American automotive engineering. The dramatic finish and the success of the Ford GT40 remain iconic, symbolizing the enduring spirit of competition and the quest for excellence in endurance racing.

<u>Dale Earnhardt's First Daytona 500 Win (1998)</u>

The Achievement:

Dale Earnhardt's victory in the 1998 Daytona 500 was a landmark moment in NASCAR history. Known as "The Intimidator" for his aggressive driving style, Earnhardt had long been a dominant force in the sport but had never won the prestigious Daytona 500 until 1998. His win was a culmination of years of near-misses and solidified his status as one of NASCAR's greatest drivers.

Context and Background:

1. Dale Earnhardt's Career:

o Early Success: Dale Earnhardt began his NASCAR career in the late 1970s and quickly established himself as a formidable driver. Known for his aggressive racing style and tenacity, he became one of the most popular and respected figures in the sport.

o Daytona 500's Elusive Victory: Despite his many accomplishments, including multiple NASCAR Cup Series championships, Earnhardt had never won the Daytona 500, one of the most coveted races in the sport. The Daytona 500 is held annually at Daytona International Speedway in Florida and is considered the crown jewel of NASCAR.

2. Pre-Race Context:

○ Earnhardt's History at Daytona: Earnhardt had come close to winning the Daytona 500 several times before 1998. He had finished in the top ten numerous times and was known for his competitive performances at the track, but victory had eluded him.

○ Team and Car: For the 1998 Daytona 500, Earnhardt drove the No. 3 Chevrolet Monte Carlo for Richard Childress Racing. The team was well-prepared and had been working diligently to secure a win at the Daytona 500.

The Race:
1. Race Day Conditions:

○ High Expectations: The 1998 Daytona 500 was anticipated to be a competitive race, with Earnhardt among the favorites. The race featured a strong field of drivers and teams, all vying for the coveted victory.

○ Strategy and Performance: Throughout the race, Earnhardt demonstrated a combination of skillful driving and strategic maneuvering. His experience and familiarity with Daytona's unique racing conditions played a crucial role in his performance.

2. Climactic Moments:

○ Final Laps: The final laps of the race were marked by intense competition and strategic racing. Earnhardt navigated through the pack, positioning himself for a chance at victory.

○ Victory: Earnhardt took the lead in the closing laps and held off the competition to win the race. His triumph was celebrated as a long-awaited achievement and a testament to his perseverance and skill.

Impact and Significance:
1. Emotional Victory:

o Long-Awaited Success: For Earnhardt, winning the Daytona 500 was a personal and professional milestone. The victory was seen as the culmination of his career-long pursuit of the race and was celebrated by fans and fellow competitors alike.

o Celebration: The win was marked by emotional celebrations, with Earnhardt's victory lap and post-race festivities reflecting the significance of the achievement. The victory was also a tribute to his dedication and hard work over the years.

2. Legacy in NASCAR:

o Career Milestone: The 1998 Daytona 500 win solidified Earnhardt's legacy as one of NASCAR's greatest drivers. It completed his list of major achievements and added a crowning moment to his illustrious career.

o Impact on Fans and the Sport: The victory resonated with fans and the broader NASCAR community, reinforcing Earnhardt's status as a beloved and iconic figure in the sport. His win at Daytona became a defining moment in NASCAR history and contributed to the ongoing legacy of his career.

3. Post-Race Influence:

○ Continued Success: Earnhardt continued to be a dominant force in NASCAR following his Daytona 500 victory. He remained a key figure in the sport and continued to compete at a high level.

○ Cultural Impact: Earnhardt's victory at Daytona became a part of NASCAR lore and was featured in various media, reflecting his impact on the sport and his place in racing history.

Conclusion:

Dale Earnhardt's first Daytona 500 win in 1998 was a historic and emotional moment in NASCAR. The victory marked the culmination of years of effort and near-misses, establishing Earnhardt as one of the sport's legends. The triumph was celebrated for its significance to Earnhardt's career, its impact on NASCAR, and its resonance with fans. The win at Daytona remains a defining moment in the history of NASCAR and a testament to Earnhardt's enduring legacy in the sport.

<u>Lewis Hamilton's 7th Formula 1 World Championship (2020)</u>

The Achievement:

Lewis Hamilton's 7th Formula 1 World Championship in 2020 tied the all-time record for the most F1 titles, held by Michael Schumacher. This monumental achievement not only underscored Hamilton's dominance in the sport but also solidified his place among the greatest drivers in Formula 1 history.

Context and Background:

1. Lewis Hamilton's Career:

○ Early Success: Hamilton entered Formula 1 in 2007 with McLaren and made an immediate impact, finishing third in his debut race and narrowly missing out on the championship in his rookie season. His skill, determination, and innovative driving style quickly made him one of the sport's leading figures.

o Previous Championships: Hamilton won his first world championship in 2008. He then went on to win additional titles in 2014, 2015, 2017, 2018, and 2019, establishing himself as a dominant force in the sport.

2. 2020 Season Context:

o COVID-19 Impact: The 2020 Formula 1 season was heavily impacted by the COVID-19 pandemic. The season was shortened, and the schedule was altered, with races being held under strict health protocols.

o Team and Car: Hamilton drove for Mercedes-AMG Petronas Formula One Team, which was the dominant team in the sport during this period. The Mercedes W11 was a highly competitive car, contributing significantly to Hamilton's success.

The Season:
1. Dominance in 2020:

o Consistent Performance: Hamilton's performance throughout the 2020 season was exceptional. He won 11 of the 17 races, showcasing his driving skill, consistency, and ability to adapt to various racing conditions.

o Notable Races: Some of Hamilton's standout performances included his wins at the British Grand Prix, Spanish Grand Prix, and Portuguese Grand Prix, where he demonstrated both his strategic prowess and sheer speed.

2. Tying the Record:

○ Championship Secured: Hamilton secured the 2020 championship with several races to spare. His win at the Turkish Grand Prix, where he clinched the title, was particularly notable for the challenging weather conditions and his remarkable ability to navigate the slippery track.

○ Record-Tying Achievement: By winning his 7th championship, Hamilton equaled Michael Schumacher's record of seven world titles, a feat that highlighted his extraordinary career and solidified his place among the sport's all-time greats.

Impact and Significance:
1. Historical Legacy:

○ Tying Schumacher's Record: Hamilton's achievement of tying Schumacher's record was a historic moment in Formula 1. Schumacher's dominance in the late 1990s and early 2000s had set a high bar, and Hamilton's ability to match that record emphasized his exceptional career.

○ Recognition and Respect: The achievement earned Hamilton widespread recognition and respect from fans, peers, and the broader motorsport community. It underscored his contributions to the sport and his enduring impact.

2. Influence on the Sport:

○ Evolution of Formula 1: Hamilton's success and dominance in the sport have contributed to the evolution of Formula 1, influencing how drivers approach the sport and how teams develop their cars. His driving style, adaptability, and strategic approach have set new standards in Formula 1 racing.

○ Diversity and Representation: Hamilton has also been a prominent advocate for diversity and inclusion in motorsport. His achievements and activism have helped raise awareness about issues related to race and representation in the sport.

3. Cultural and Social Impact:

○ Role Model: Hamilton's success and public presence have made him a role model for aspiring athletes and a prominent figure in popular culture. His achievements extend beyond the racetrack, influencing various aspects of society and inspiring a new generation of fans and drivers.

○ Legacy in Formula 1: Hamilton's legacy in Formula 1 is defined by his record-tying championships, his impact on the sport's evolution, and his contributions to important social issues. His career will be remembered as one of the most influential in the history of motorsport.

Conclusion:

Lewis Hamilton's 7th Formula 1 World Championship in 2020 was a landmark achievement that tied the record for the most titles in Formula 1 history. His dominance during the season, combined with his exceptional driving skills and strategic acumen, solidified his place among the sport's greatest drivers. The achievement not only highlighted Hamilton's remarkable career but also had a lasting impact on Formula 1, contributing to the sport's evolution and influencing its cultural and social landscape.

Chapter 13: Unforgettable Team Triumphs

<u>Mia Hamm Leads U.S. to World Cup Victory (1999)</u>

The Achievement:

Mia Hamm's performance in the 1999 FIFA Women's World Cup was a defining moment for women's soccer. Hamm, a key player for the U.S. Women's National Team (USWNT), led the team to victory in a tournament that became a landmark event for women's sports. The final, played at the Rose Bowl in Pasadena, California, was a pivotal moment in the history of women's soccer.

Context and Background:

1. Mia Hamm's Career:

   o Early Achievements: Mia Hamm began her international career in 1987 and quickly established herself as one of the world's top players. Known for her speed, skill, and leadership, Hamm became a prominent figure in women's soccer.

   o Previous Success: Before the 1999 World Cup, Hamm and the USWNT had already achieved considerable success, including winning the inaugural Women's World Cup in 1991 and securing gold medals at the 1996 Atlanta Olympics.

2. 1999 FIFA Women's World Cup:

   o Tournament Overview: The 1999 Women's World Cup was held in the United States from June 10 to July 10. It was the second edition of the tournament and featured 16 teams competing in various cities across the country.

○ Growing Popularity: The tournament was a crucial moment for the growth of women's soccer, with increased media coverage and attendance, marking a significant step forward for women's sports.

The Tournament:
1. USWNT's Journey:

○ Group Stage: The USWNT performed strongly in the group stage, winning all three of their matches and showcasing their skill and teamwork.

○ Knockout Rounds: In the knockout stages, the team continued to impress with solid performances, including a memorable 3-0 win over Germany in the semifinals.

2. The Final Match:

○ The Match: The final was held on July 10, 1999, at the Rose Bowl in Pasadena, California, where the USWNT faced China in a highly anticipated showdown.

○ The Game: The match ended in a 0-0 draw after regular and extra time, leading to a penalty shootout. The USWNT emerged victorious, winning the shootout 5-4. Hamm, along with her teammates, played a crucial role in the team's performance throughout the tournament.

Impact and Significance:
1. Boosting Women's Soccer:

o Increased Visibility: The 1999 World Cup final was watched by over 90,000 spectators at the Rose Bowl and by millions more on television, bringing unprecedented visibility to women's soccer.

o Cultural Impact: The victory was a watershed moment for women's sports, inspiring young athletes and elevating the profile of women's soccer both in the U.S. and internationally.

2. Mia Hamm's Legacy:

o Leadership and Influence: Hamm's leadership and exceptional performance throughout the tournament cemented her status as one of the greatest female soccer players of all time. Her influence extended beyond the field, as she became a prominent advocate for women's sports and gender equality.

o Role Model: Hamm's success provided a powerful role model for aspiring female athletes and demonstrated the potential for women's sports to achieve high levels of success and recognition.

3. Long-Term Impact:

o Growth of Women's Soccer: The 1999 World Cup played a significant role in the growth of women's soccer, leading to increased investment, development, and support for women's teams and leagues around the world.

o Legacy of the USWNT: The victory established the USWNT as a dominant force in women's soccer and set the stage for continued success in subsequent tournaments.

The team's achievements in 1999 paved the way for future victories and continued growth of the sport.

Conclusion:

Mia Hamm's leadership in the 1999 FIFA Women's World Cup was a pivotal moment for women's soccer. The USWNT's victory not only marked a historic achievement in the sport but also had a profound impact on the visibility and growth of women's sports. Hamm's exceptional performance and the team's success provided a lasting legacy that continues to inspire and shape the world of women's soccer. The 1999 World Cup remains a landmark event, celebrating the potential and achievements of female athletes and advancing the recognition of women's sports on a global stage.

<u>The "Music City Miracle" (2000)</u>

The Achievement:

The "Music City Miracle" is one of the most memorable and dramatic plays in NFL history. This stunning play, executed by the Tennessee Titans during the AFC Wild Card playoff game against the Buffalo Bills on January 8, 2000, secured a last-minute victory for the Titans and is celebrated for its high stakes and incredible execution.

Context and Background:

1. The Teams:

   o Tennessee Titans: The Titans, then known as the Houston Oilers before relocating to Tennessee, had a solid season in 1999 and were making a significant playoff push. Under head coach Jeff Fisher, they had a strong roster, including star running back Eddie George and quarterback Steve McNair.

   o Buffalo Bills: The Bills, coached by Wade Phillips, were a formidable team with a strong defense and a high-powered offense led by quarterback Rob Johnson. They were looking to advance in the playoffs after a successful regular season.

2. The Playoff Situation:

○ AFC Wild Card Game: The game was held at Nashville's Adelphia Coliseum. The Titans were trailing the Bills 16-15 with just 16 seconds remaining in the game, making their situation critical as they needed a big play to turn the game around.

The Play:
1. The Setup:

○ Kickoff Return: With 16 seconds left in the game, the Titans were preparing to receive a kickoff from the Bills. The kickoff was crucial as it would determine if the Titans could manage a final play to attempt a victory.

2. The Execution:

○ The Lateral Play: On the kickoff, Titans' return man Lorenzo Neal received the ball and immediately handed it off to tight end Frank Wycheck. Wycheck then threw a lateral pass across the field to wide receiver Kevin Dyson.

○ Dyson's Run: Dyson, after catching the lateral, ran down the sideline for a 75-yard touchdown. His run was a dramatic and electrifying finish, giving the Titans a 22-16 victory.

Impact and Significance:
1. Immediate Impact:

○ Game-Winning Play: The "Music City Miracle" allowed the Titans to advance to the next round of the playoffs, defeating the Bills in one of the most thrilling finishes in NFL history.

○ Historical Significance: The play is notable not only for its dramatic timing but also for its execution and impact on the outcome of the game.

2. Legacy:

○ Iconic Moment: The "Music City Miracle" has become one of the most iconic plays in NFL history, often cited as a prime example of a game-changing moment and a remarkable display of teamwork and creativity.

○ Cultural Impact: The play remains a celebrated moment in sports, symbolizing the unpredictable and thrilling nature of football. It has been featured in numerous highlight reels and is a memorable part of the Titans' and NFL lore.

3. Controversy and Discussion:

○ Rules and Controversy: The play has been the subject of controversy and debate, particularly regarding the legality of the lateral pass. Despite the debate, it has been officially recognized as a valid play by the NFL.

Conclusion:

The "Music City Miracle" stands as a testament to the excitement and unpredictability of football. This dramatic play, executed flawlessly by the Tennessee Titans, is celebrated for its incredible timing, creativity, and impact on the game. It secured a memorable playoff victory for the Titans and remains a defining moment in NFL history, highlighting the thrilling nature of sports and the enduring legacy of remarkable plays.

Larry Bird's 60-Point Game (1985)

The Achievement:

Larry Bird's 60-point game on March 12, 1985, is one of the most extraordinary individual performances in NBA history. As a member of the Boston Celtics, Bird's remarkable scoring display exemplified his legendary skill, competitiveness, and impact on the game of basketball.

Context and Background:

1. Larry Bird's Career:

○ Early Years: Larry Bird, known for his exceptional shooting, passing, and basketball IQ, had already established himself as one of the NBA's premier players by the mid-1980s. He was a three-time NBA Champion (1981, 1984, 1986), a three-time MVP (1984, 1985, 1986), and a key figure in the Celtics' storied history.

○ 1984-1985 Season: The 1984-1985 NBA season was another standout year for Bird, as he continued to lead the Celtics with his scoring ability and all-around play. His team was in contention for the top spot in the Eastern Conference and aimed for another championship run.

2. The Opponent and the Game:

○ Boston Celtics vs. Atlanta Hawks: The Celtics faced the Atlanta Hawks at the Boston Garden. The Hawks were a competitive team, and the matchup was crucial for both teams' playoff positioning.

○ Game Context: The Celtics were in need of a significant performance to secure a win and strengthen their position in the standings. Bird's scoring prowess would play a pivotal role in achieving this goal.

The Performance:

1. Dominant Scoring:

○ First Half: Bird started the game with a strong performance, scoring efficiently and demonstrating his exceptional shooting ability. By halftime, he had already amassed a significant portion of his eventual total.

○ Second Half: Bird's scoring exploded in the second half as he continued to dominate offensively. He scored 32 points in the second half alone, showcasing his versatility and clutch ability.

2. Historic Outcome:

○ Final Statistics: Bird finished the game with a career-high 60 points on 22-of-36 shooting, including 6-of-10 from three-point range. He also added 7 rebounds, 3 assists, and 2 steals, contributing significantly to the Celtics' 120-104 victory over the Hawks.

○ Significance: Bird's 60-point game was the highest single-game scoring performance of his career and one of the highest in Celtics history. It also cemented his reputation as one of the most prolific scorers in NBA history.

Impact and Significance:

1. Impact on the Celtics:

○ Team Success: Bird's performance was crucial for the Celtics' victory, and his scoring outburst helped them secure a win in a critical matchup. His leadership and offensive firepower were essential for the team's success.

○ Team Chemistry: The game further solidified Bird's role as the leader of the Celtics and highlighted his ability to perform under pressure.

2. Legacy and Influence:

○ Historical Context: Bird's 60-point game is remembered as one of the greatest individual performances in NBA history. It is a testament to his scoring ability, consistency, and impact on the game.

○ Influence on Future Players: Bird's performance has inspired countless players to strive for excellence in scoring and has become a benchmark for high-scoring games in the league. His ability to excel in high-pressure situations remains a model for future generations.

3. Cultural Impact:

○ NBA Lore: The game is often cited in discussions of the greatest individual performances in NBA history. It is celebrated for its display of skill, precision, and competitive spirit.

○ Bird's Legacy: Larry Bird's 60-point game is a defining moment in his illustrious career and contributes to his enduring legacy as one of the greatest players in basketball history.

Conclusion:

Larry Bird's 60-point game in 1985 is a landmark achievement in NBA history, showcasing his exceptional scoring ability and competitive drive. The performance was a career-high and a key moment in the Celtics' successful season. Bird's remarkable display of talent and skill in this game further solidified his legacy as one of the greatest players in the history of basketball and remains a celebrated moment in the sport's rich history.

Chapter 14: Moments That Redefined Sports

<u>Wayne Gretzky's 50 Goals in 39 Games (1981-82)</u>

The Achievement:

Wayne Gretzky's remarkable feat of scoring 50 goals in just 39 games during the 1981-82 NHL season stands as one of the most extraordinary accomplishments in hockey history. This achievement not only highlighted Gretzky's unparalleled skill and scoring prowess but also redefined the expectations for goal-scoring in the NHL.

Context and Background:

1. Wayne Gretzky's Career:

○ Early Years: Known as "The Great One," Wayne Gretzky had already established himself as a hockey prodigy by the early 1980s. His vision, passing, and goal-scoring ability set him apart as one of the most dominant players in the league.

○ NHL Debut: Gretzky made his NHL debut with the Edmonton Oilers in 1979. By the 1981-82 season, he was well-established as a top player, having already won the Hart Trophy as the NHL's Most Valuable Player in each of his first two seasons.

2. 1981-82 NHL Season:

○ Team Context: The Edmonton Oilers, with Gretzky as their centerpiece, were emerging as a dominant force in the NHL. The 1981-82 season was pivotal as the Oilers were building towards their dynasty years.

○ Goal-Scoring Expectations: The standard for goal-scoring in the NHL was high, but Gretzky's ability to exceed these expectations set a new benchmark for offensive performance.

The Performance:
1. Record-Breaking Pace:

○ Early Success: Gretzky's goal-scoring began at a blistering pace. By mid-November, he was already on a trajectory that hinted at his eventual record-breaking achievement.

○ Historical Context: The previous record for fastest to 50 goals was held by Maurice Richard, who scored 50 goals in 50 games. Gretzky's pace would not only break this record but also set a new standard.

2. The 39-Game Achievement:

○ Game-by-Game: Gretzky scored his 50th goal of the season on December 30, 1981, in a game against the Philadelphia Flyers. He achieved this milestone in just 39 games, surpassing Richard's 50-in-50 record.

○ Scoring Prowess: Gretzky's 50 goals included a mix of power plays, even-strength goals, and some spectacular individual efforts. His exceptional ability to find the net from various positions on the ice underscored his scoring versatility.

Impact and Significance:
1. Impact on the NHL:

○ Record-Setting Achievement: Gretzky's feat of scoring 50 goals in 39 games remains one of the most celebrated records in NHL history. It set a new standard for goal-scoring excellence and showcased Gretzky's unparalleled skill.

○ Impact on Opponents: The record also had a psychological impact on opponents, as it demonstrated the difficulty of defending against one of the greatest players in the sport's history.

2. Legacy and Influence:

○ Historical Legacy: This achievement further cemented Gretzky's status as one of the greatest players in hockey history. His ability to score at such an incredible pace is a testament to his skill, preparation, and understanding of the game.

○ Influence on Future Generations: Gretzky's record has inspired countless players to push the boundaries of goal-scoring. His performance has become a benchmark for aspiring hockey players and is often cited in discussions of the greatest individual accomplishments in sports.

3. Cultural Impact:

○ NHL Lore: Gretzky's 50 goals in 39 games is a defining moment in NHL history and is frequently highlighted in discussions of the sport's greatest achievements. It is a symbol of Gretzky's impact on the game and his role as a transformative figure in hockey.

○ Enduring Legacy: The achievement remains a powerful symbol of Gretzky's dominance and skill. It continues to be celebrated by fans and analysts as one of the greatest individual accomplishments in the history of professional sports.

Conclusion:

Wayne Gretzky's 50 goals in 39 games during the 1981-82 NHL season is an extraordinary milestone that stands as a testament to his exceptional talent and scoring ability. The achievement redefined the expectations for goal-scoring in hockey and solidified Gretzky's legacy as one of the greatest players in the sport's history. His record-breaking performance remains a celebrated moment in NHL history, embodying his influence on the game and inspiring future generations of hockey players.

<u>Bob Beamon's Long Jump Record (1968)</u>

The Achievement:

Bob Beamon's long jump at the 1968 Mexico City Olympics is one of the most iconic moments in track and field history. His jump of 8.90 meters (29 feet, 2½ inches) set a world record that would stand for 23 years, and it is celebrated not only for its incredible distance but also for its impact on the sport and its historical context.

Context and Background:

1. Bob Beamon's Career:

o Early Life and Training: Born on March 9, 1946, in Jamaica, New York, Beamon began his athletic career in high school before joining the University of Texas at El Paso, where he became a standout in track and field. His natural ability and rigorous training laid the groundwork for his future success.

o Previous Achievements: By the time of the 1968 Olympics, Beamon had already established himself as a top competitor, with notable performances in national and international events. However, his long jump at the Mexico City Games would elevate him to legendary status.

2. 1968 Mexico City Olympics:

○ Olympic Context: The 1968 Olympics were held in Mexico City, notable for its high altitude, which provided athletes with advantageous conditions due to the reduced air resistance. The games were also marked by significant social and political turmoil, adding to the drama and significance of the events.

○ Long Jump Competition: The long jump was one of the premier field events, and Beamon's performance was highly anticipated. The field included some of the world's best jumpers, but Beamon's leap would prove to be extraordinary.

The Performance:
1. Record-Breaking Jump:

○ The Moment: On October 18, 1968, during the long jump final, Beamon made his historic jump on his fourth attempt. His leap of 8.90 meters was far beyond the previous world record of 8.35 meters (27 feet, 4¾ inches) held by Soviet jumper Igor Ter-Ovanesyan.

○ Technological and Measurement Issues: Beamon's jump was so far beyond expectations that it initially caused confusion. The measurement was delayed as officials recalibrated the measuring devices. Beamon's jump not only shattered the previous record but also exceeded the expectations of many in the sport.

2. The Impact of the Jump:

○ Record Impact: Beamon's jump was more than just a new world record; it was a dramatic improvement over the previous mark. The 55-centimeter (21½-inch) increase was unprecedented and highlighted the extent of Beamon's athleticism.

○ Visual and Emotional Impact: Beamon's leap was visually striking and emotionally resonant. The jump was a testament to his explosive power and technique, and it left an indelible mark on the sport.

Impact and Significance:
1. Transformative Achievement:

○ Sporting Impact: Beamon's record was so extraordinary that it revolutionized the long jump. It set a new standard for the event and challenged other competitors to push their limits. The jump was not just a record; it was a redefining moment for the sport.

○ Cultural Impact: Beamon's performance occurred during a period of social and political upheaval, and his achievement provided a moment of inspiration and unity. It was seen as a triumph of human potential and excellence.

2. Legacy in Track and Field:

○ Enduring Record: Beamon's record stood for 23 years, until it was surpassed by Mike Powell in 1991. The longevity of the record highlighted the exceptional nature of Beamon's achievement.

○ Influence on Athletes: Beamon's jump inspired a generation of athletes to push the boundaries of what was possible in the long jump. His performance is often cited as one of the greatest individual achievements in Olympic history.

3. Cultural and Historical Impact:

○ Symbol of Excellence: Beamon's long jump became a symbol of excellence and possibility. It demonstrated the potential of human achievement and the impact of combining talent with hard work and determination.

○ Historical Significance: The 1968 Olympics were notable for their political and social context, and Beamon's jump provided a positive and memorable highlight. His achievement is remembered as a beacon of athletic prowess and a moment of triumph.

Conclusion:

Bob Beamon's long jump at the 1968 Mexico City Olympics is a defining moment in the history of track and field. His extraordinary leap of 8.90 meters not only set a world record but also redefined the possibilities of the long jump. Beamon's performance remains a celebrated and influential achievement in sports history, symbolizing the peak of athletic excellence and the enduring impact of remarkable accomplishments. His jump continues to inspire and resonate as one of the most memorable moments in Olympic history.

Simone Biles' 2016 Olympic Dominance

The Achievement:

Simone Biles' performance at the 2016 Rio de Janeiro Olympics was a historic display of gymnastics prowess, marking a new standard for the sport. Biles won four gold medals and one bronze, showcasing a level of skill, precision, and artistry that redefined gymnastics.

Context and Background:

1. Simone Biles' Career Up to 2016:

○ Early Life and Training: Born on March 14, 1997, in Columbus, Ohio, Simone Biles began gymnastics at a young age. Her prodigious talent was evident early on, leading her to a rigorous training regimen under coach Aimee Boorman.

○ Previous Achievements: Before the 2016 Olympics, Biles had already made a significant impact in gymnastics. She won multiple titles at the World Championships, including being a three-time World All-Around Champion (2013, 2014, 2015), setting the stage for her Olympic success.

2. 2016 Rio de Janeiro Olympics:

○ Olympic Context: The Rio Olympics were held from August 5 to August 21, 2016. The gymnastics events were particularly anticipated, with Biles as one of the standout athletes due to her remarkable performances leading up to the Games.

○ Competition: Biles faced strong competition from other elite gymnasts, but her combination of technical skill, difficulty, and execution made her a favorite to dominate the event.

The Performance:
1. Record-Breaking and Gold Medal Victories:

○ Team Competition: On August 9, 2016, Biles led the U.S. women's gymnastics team to victory in the team competition. The "Final Five" (Biles, Aly Raisman, Gabby Douglas, Laurie Hernandez, and Madison Kocian) won gold with a dominant performance, showcasing a wide range of skills and routines.

○ Individual All-Around: On August 11, Biles won the individual all-around gold medal with a score of 62.198, a significant margin ahead of second place. Her routines were praised for their high difficulty and flawless execution.

○ Vault: On August 14, Biles won gold in the vault final, performing a Yurchenko double pike and a Cheng, both of which were performed with exceptional precision.

○ Balance Beam: On August 15, Biles secured gold on the balance beam, delivering a performance marked by her signature strength and grace, despite a slight wobble.

○ Floor Exercise: On August 16, Biles won her final gold medal in the floor exercise, where she executed a routine with complex tumbling passes and expressive choreography. Her performance was both technically superior and artistically captivating.

○ Bronze Medal: In addition to her gold medals, Biles earned a bronze in the uneven bars final, adding to her impressive tally.

2. Historic Significance:

○ Skill and Difficulty: Biles' performances featured groundbreaking elements and routines, including the introduction of skills named after her (e.g., the "Biles" on floor exercise). Her routines pushed the boundaries of what was possible in gymnastics, with a combination of difficulty and execution that set new standards.

○ Dominance: Her four gold medals and one bronze were a testament to her dominance in the sport. Biles' ability to perform under the pressure of the Olympic stage and execute complex routines with near-perfection was unprecedented.

Impact and Significance:
1. Redefining Gymnastics:

○ Technical Innovation: Biles' routines introduced new elements and set new records in difficulty. Her performances highlighted the evolving nature of gymnastics and inspired changes in the sport's technical standards.

○ Performance Standards: Biles' dominance established a new benchmark for gymnastics performances. Her ability to perform at such a high level across multiple events showcased a level of versatility and skill that redefined the sport.

2. Cultural and Inspirational Impact:

○ Role Model: Biles became an inspirational figure for young athletes, particularly women and girls. Her achievements in gymnastics demonstrated the possibilities of dedication, hard work, and perseverance.

○ Media and Popularity: Biles' success at the Rio Olympics garnered widespread media attention and increased the popularity of gymnastics. Her charisma and excellence brought new fans to the sport and heightened its visibility on a global scale.

3. Legacy and Influence:

○ Continued Success: Biles' 2016 Olympic success solidified her status as one of the greatest gymnasts of all time. Her influence extended beyond the Rio Games, with continued success in subsequent competitions and her impact on the sport's future.

○ Changing the Sport: Biles' achievements prompted discussions about the evolution of gymnastics and the increasing difficulty of routines. Her performances inspired future generations of gymnasts to push the limits of their capabilities.

Conclusion:

Simone Biles' 2016 Olympic dominance was a landmark moment in gymnastics history. Her four gold medals and one bronze, coupled with her innovative routines and flawless execution, redefined the sport and set new standards for excellence. Biles' achievements in Rio de Janeiro demonstrated extraordinary skill, determination, and grace, establishing her as one of the greatest gymnasts of all time. Her legacy continues to inspire and influence the world of gymnastics and beyond.

Chapter 15: Iconic Moments of Skill and Precision

<u>Wayne Gretzky's Record-Breaking Career</u>

The Achievement:

Wayne Gretzky, often referred to as "The Great One," is widely regarded as the greatest hockey player in history. His career is marked by numerous records and achievements that set him apart from his peers and defined the sport of hockey. Gretzky's unmatched accomplishments include records for career goals, assists, points, and more, making him a legend in the NHL and beyond.

Context and Background:

1. Early Life and Career Beginnings:

o Early Life: Born on January 26, 1961, in Brantford, Ontario, Wayne Gretzky displayed exceptional hockey talent from a young age. His early years in minor hockey showcased his skill, vision, and understanding of the game.

o Junior and Professional Debut: Gretzky played in the Ontario Hockey League (OHL) and then joined the World Hockey Association (WHA) with the Indianapolis Racers and later the Edmonton Oilers. His success in the WHA led to his transition to the NHL in 1979 when the WHA-NHL merger occurred.

2. NHL Career Overview:

o Teams: Gretzky played for the Edmonton Oilers, Los Angeles Kings, St. Louis Blues, and New York Rangers during his NHL career.

○ Career Span: His NHL career spanned from 1979 to 1999, during which he consistently performed at an elite level and set numerous records.

Record-Breaking Achievements:
1. Career Records:

○ Goals: Gretzky holds the NHL record for career goals with 894. This record is remarkable not only for its total but also for the consistency with which Gretzky scored throughout his career.

○ Assists: He also holds the record for career assists with 1,963. Gretzky's vision and playmaking ability allowed him to set up countless goals for his teammates.

○ Points: With 2,857 career points, Gretzky's combined total of goals and assists remains unmatched. This record underscores his all-around offensive capabilities.

○ Single-Season Records: Gretzky holds the record for most goals in a single season (92 in 1981-82), most assists in a single season (163 in 1985-86), and most points in a single season (215 in 1985-86).

○ Consecutive Scoring Titles: He won the Art Ross Trophy as the league's leading scorer for 10 consecutive seasons from 1980-81 to 1989-90, a testament to his sustained excellence.

2. Playoff Records:

○ Stanley Cup Championships: Gretzky led the Edmonton Oilers to four consecutive Stanley Cup championships from

1984 to 1987, further cementing his legacy as a clutch performer.

○ Playoff Points: He holds the record for career playoff points with 382, showcasing his ability to perform in high-pressure situations.

Impact and Significance:
1. Redefining Hockey:

○ Skill and Vision: Gretzky's exceptional skill, vision, and hockey IQ transformed the way the game was played. His ability to anticipate plays, make precise passes, and score goals set new standards for offensive play.

○ Influence on the Game: Gretzky's impact on hockey extended beyond his playing career. His style of play, leadership, and success influenced future generations of players and contributed to the evolution of the sport.

2. Cultural and Inspirational Impact:

○ Global Popularity: Gretzky's success helped popularize hockey in the United States and around the world. His presence in the NHL brought increased attention to the sport and inspired countless young players.

○ Role Model: As a player known for his work ethic, sportsmanship, and dedication, Gretzky became a role model for athletes across various sports. His achievements demonstrated the rewards of hard work and perseverance.

3. Legacy and Recognition:

○ Hall of Fame: Gretzky was inducted into the Hockey Hall of Fame in 1999, a testament to his contributions to the sport.

○ Awards and Honors: Throughout his career, Gretzky received numerous awards and honors, including the Hart Trophy as the NHL's Most Valuable Player (MVP) multiple times, and he was named to the NHL All-Star Team many times.

Conclusion:

Wayne Gretzky's career is defined by unmatched achievements and records that set him apart as the greatest hockey player of all time. His career goals, assists, and points records, along with his impact on the game and his role as an ambassador for hockey, have left a lasting legacy. Gretzky's influence extends beyond the rink, inspiring future generations and shaping the sport of hockey in profound ways. His contributions to the game and his remarkable career accomplishments ensure that his place in sports history remains unparalleled.

<u>Secretariat's Triple Crown</u>

The Achievement:

Secretariat's Triple Crown victory in 1973 remains one of the most dominant performances in the history of horse racing. His triumphs in the Kentucky Derby, the Preakness Stakes, and the Belmont Stakes not only cemented his place in racing history but also showcased an extraordinary display of speed, power, and endurance.

Context and Background:

1. The Triple Crown:

   o Overview: The Triple Crown is a prestigious series of three horse races for three-year-olds in the United States: the Kentucky Derby, the Preakness Stakes, and the Belmont Stakes. Winning all three races in the same year is a rare and remarkable achievement.

   o Historical Context: By 1973, only 11 horses had won the Triple Crown since its inception in 1919. The feat is incredibly challenging due to the different distances and racing conditions of each race.

2. Secretariat's Background:

   o Early Life: Secretariat was foaled on March 30, 1970, at Meadow Stud in Doswell, Virginia. His pedigree and early performances indicated great potential, and he quickly became a standout horse in the racing community.

   o Training and Preparation: Trained by Lucien Laurin and ridden by jockey Ron Turcotte, Secretariat's preparation for the Triple Crown was meticulous. His training regimen focused on building speed and endurance, essential for the demanding series of races.

The Triple Crown Races:

1. Kentucky Derby (May 5, 1973):

o Performance: Secretariat's performance in the Kentucky Derby was remarkable. He won the race by 2 ½ lengths, finishing with a time of 1:59 2/5, a record that still stands. His powerful and smooth running style impressed spectators and established him as a horse to watch.

o Impact: Secretariat's victory in the Derby set the stage for his pursuit of the Triple Crown and generated excitement and anticipation for the subsequent races.

2. Preakness Stakes (May 19, 1973):

o Performance: In the Preakness Stakes, Secretariat continued his dominant performance. He won by 2 ½ lengths with a time of 1:54 2/5, setting a new record for the race. His speed and agility were evident as he effortlessly outpaced the competition.

o Impact: The win solidified Secretariat's status as a strong contender for the Triple Crown and increased public interest in his pursuit of racing history.

3. Belmont Stakes (June 9, 1973):

o Performance: Secretariat's performance in the Belmont Stakes was legendary. He won by 31 lengths, an unprecedented margin, with a time of 2:24 for the 1 ½ mile race. This time remains the fastest in Belmont Stakes history and showcased Secretariat's extraordinary speed and stamina.

o Impact: The sheer dominance of Secretariat's Belmont win made headlines and further cemented his place in racing lore. His performance was described as one of the greatest feats in sports history.

Impact and Significance:
1. Dominance in Horse Racing:

o Unmatched Performance: Secretariat's Triple Crown victory is celebrated for its dominance and excellence. His records in the Derby and the Belmont Stakes remain unbroken, highlighting his exceptional ability and endurance.

o Historical Significance: Secretariat's achievements set a new standard in horse racing and remain a benchmark for future generations of racehorses.

2. Cultural Impact:

o Legendary Status: Secretariat's Triple Crown win elevated him to legendary status, capturing the imagination of racing fans and the general public. His story has been celebrated in books, documentaries, and films, contributing to his enduring legacy.

o Inspiration: Secretariat's success inspired fans and aspiring racehorses, demonstrating the possibilities of greatness and the impact of extraordinary talent and training.

3. Legacy in Racing:

○ Influence on the Sport: Secretariat's performance has influenced the way horse racing is approached and appreciated. His achievements are a testament to the potential for greatness in the sport and continue to be a point of reference for future Triple Crown hopefuls.

○ Enduring Records: The records set by Secretariat, including his Belmont Stakes time and Kentucky Derby performance, remain as benchmarks of excellence in horse racing.

Conclusion:

Secretariat's Triple Crown victory in 1973 stands as one of the most dominant performances in the history of horse racing. His record-breaking times and unprecedented margin of victory in the Belmont Stakes showcased an extraordinary level of talent, speed, and endurance. Secretariat's achievements have left a lasting impact on the sport, inspiring future generations and securing his place as one of the greatest racehorses of all time. His legacy continues to be celebrated, and his remarkable performances remain a high point in the history of horse racing.

<u>Lionel Messi's Solo Goal Against Getafe (2007)</u>

The Achievement:

Lionel Messi's solo goal against Getafe in the Copa del Rey semi-final on April 18, 2007, is one of the most iconic and memorable goals in soccer history. The goal demonstrated Messi's exceptional dribbling skills, agility, and ability to perform under pressure, further solidifying his reputation as one of the greatest players of all time.

Context and Background:

1. The 2006-2007 Season:

○ Barcelona's Form: During the 2006-2007 season, FC Barcelona was a formidable team in Spanish and European football, featuring a squad filled with talent. Messi, then just 19 years old, was emerging as a key player for the club.

○ Messi's Rising Star: By 2007, Messi had already shown glimpses of his extraordinary talent, but the goal against Getafe was a defining moment in his career. It was a season where Messi was beginning to transition from a promising young talent to an established star.

2. The Copa del Rey:

○ Tournament Overview: The Copa del Rey is Spain's premier domestic cup competition, involving teams from all tiers of Spanish football. The semi-final match between Barcelona and Getafe was highly anticipated, with both teams vying for a place in the final.

○ The Stage: The match was played at the Camp Nou, Barcelona's home stadium, providing Messi with a familiar and supportive environment.

The Goal:
1. The Build-Up:

○ The Moment: In the 87th minute of the match, with the score tied at 1-1, Barcelona needed a decisive play to secure victory. Messi picked up the ball in his own half and began his mesmerizing run.

○ The Dribble: Messi embarked on a solo run from just inside his own half, evading multiple Getafe defenders with his exceptional dribbling skills. His low center of gravity and close ball control allowed him to navigate through tight spaces and maintain possession.

2. The Execution:

o The Finish: After weaving past several defenders, Messi reached the edge of the penalty area and slotted the ball past the Getafe goalkeeper with a precise finish. The goal was reminiscent of Diego Maradona's famous "Goal of the Century" against England in the 1986 World Cup, showcasing Messi's ability to execute a similar feat with his unique style.

o The Reaction: Messi's goal was met with thunderous applause from the Camp Nou crowd and was widely praised by fans, pundits, and fellow players for its brilliance and artistry.

Impact and Significance:
1. Showcasing Messi's Brilliance:

o Technical Mastery: The goal exemplified Messi's technical proficiency, dribbling ability, and composure under pressure. His ability to navigate through a crowd of defenders and finish with precision highlighted his exceptional skill set.

o Comparisons to Maradona: The goal drew comparisons to Diego Maradona's iconic solo effort in the 1986 World Cup, further cementing Messi's place in soccer's pantheon of greats.

2. Cultural and Soccer Impact:

o Global Recognition: Messi's goal against Getafe was broadcasted worldwide and became one of the defining moments of his early career. It contributed to his growing reputation as one of the best players in the world.

○ Inspiration: The goal served as an inspiration to young players and soccer enthusiasts, demonstrating the beauty and creativity that can be achieved on the field.

3. Legacy:

○ Career Milestone: The goal is often cited as a pivotal moment in Messi's career, showcasing his potential to become one of the greatest players in history. It is frequently featured in highlight reels and discussions of his best moments.

○ Influence on Soccer: Messi's solo goal against Getafe remains a benchmark for individual brilliance in soccer. It is a reminder of the magic that can happen in football and the extraordinary talents that can transform a match.

Conclusion:
Lionel Messi's solo goal against Getafe in 2007 is a shining example of his exceptional talent and creativity on the soccer field. The goal, with its breathtaking dribbling and precise finish, solidified Messi's reputation as one of the greatest players in soccer history. Its impact extends beyond the match itself, inspiring fans and players alike and contributing to Messi's legacy as a football icon.

Chapter 16: The Next Generation of Greatness

Patrick Mahomes' Super Bowl LIV Performance (2020)

The Achievement:

Patrick Mahomes' performance in Super Bowl LIV, held on February 2, 2020, is one of the most remarkable and memorable in NFL history. Leading the Kansas City Chiefs to a 31-20 victory over the San Francisco 49ers, Mahomes orchestrated a dramatic comeback that secured his first Super Bowl title and the Chiefs' first in 50 years.

Context and Background:

1. Mahomes' Career Prior to Super Bowl LIV:

o Early Success: Patrick Mahomes was drafted by the Kansas City Chiefs as the 10th overall pick in the 2017 NFL Draft. By his second season (2018), he had established himself as one of the league's top quarterbacks, winning the NFL MVP award.

o Playoff Performance: The 2019 season saw Mahomes leading the Chiefs to a 12-4 record and another strong playoff performance. The Chiefs won the AFC Championship and advanced to their first Super Bowl since Super Bowl IV.

2. The Super Bowl LIV:

o Teams and Matchup: The Kansas City Chiefs faced the San Francisco 49ers at the Hard Rock Stadium in Miami Gardens, Florida. The 49ers, led by head coach Kyle

Shanahan and quarterback Jimmy Garoppolo, were considered a formidable opponent.

○ Game Context: The Chiefs entered the game as underdogs, with many experts predicting a close contest. The 49ers had a strong defense and a balanced offensive attack, making them a tough challenge for the Chiefs.

The Performance:
1. First Three Quarters:

○ Struggles: For much of the game, Mahomes and the Chiefs' offense struggled against the 49ers' defensive schemes. The 49ers built a 20-10 lead with about seven minutes remaining in the fourth quarter.

○ Pressure and Poise: Despite the challenges, Mahomes remained composed and focused, demonstrating his ability to perform under pressure.

2. The Comeback:

○ Game-Changing Plays: In the final minutes of the game, Mahomes led the Chiefs on a series of critical drives. His ability to make crucial throws and keep plays alive with his mobility proved instrumental.

○ Key Moments:

▪ Drive to Tie the Game: Mahomes threw a 44-yard completion to Tyreek Hill on a key third down, setting up a 1-yard touchdown run by Damien Williams that cut the 49ers' lead to 20-17.

- Go-Ahead Touchdown: With less than three minutes remaining, Mahomes connected with Travis Kelce for a 1-yard touchdown pass, giving the Chiefs a 24-20 lead.

- Final Score: Damien Williams sealed the victory with a 38-yard touchdown run, bringing the final score to 31-20.

Impact and Significance:
1. Mahomes' Legacy:

○ Young Star: At just 24 years old, Mahomes' performance in Super Bowl LIV established him as one of the premier quarterbacks in the NFL. His ability to lead a comeback and deliver under pressure was a testament to his skill and poise.

○ Historic Achievement: Mahomes became the youngest quarterback to win the Super Bowl MVP award and the second African-American quarterback to win a Super Bowl, following Doug Williams.

2. Kansas City Chiefs:

○ Breaking the Drought: The Chiefs' victory in Super Bowl LIV ended a 50-year championship drought for the franchise, marking a significant moment in the team's history.

○ Cultural Impact: The win revitalized the Kansas City Chiefs' fan base and elevated the team's status in the NFL. The victory parade and celebrations demonstrated the deep connection between the team and its supporters.

3. NFL Impact:

○ Influence on the Game: Mahomes' performance showcased the evolving nature of the quarterback position, highlighting the importance of mobility, improvisation, and big-play ability. His style of play and leadership qualities have inspired a new generation of quarterbacks.

○ Media and Fan Attention: Mahomes' success has garnered widespread media attention and increased fan interest in the NFL. His charismatic personality and dynamic play have made him one of the league's most marketable stars.

Conclusion:

Patrick Mahomes' performance in Super Bowl LIV was a defining moment in his career and in NFL history. Leading the Kansas City Chiefs to a dramatic comeback victory, Mahomes demonstrated his exceptional talent, resilience, and leadership. His performance not only secured the Chiefs' first Super Bowl title in five decades but also solidified his status as one of the game's brightest stars. The impact of his performance extends beyond the game itself, influencing the NFL and inspiring fans and players alike.

Giannis Antetokounmpo's 50-Point Game in NBA Finals (2021)

The Achievement:

Giannis Antetokounmpo's performance in Game 6 of the 2021 NBA Finals was one of the most remarkable individual displays in NBA history. Scoring 50 points, Antetokounmpo led the Milwaukee Bucks to a 105-98 victory over the Phoenix Suns, securing their first NBA Championship in 50 years.

Context and Background:

1. Antetokounmpo's Career Prior to the 2021 Finals:

○ Rise to Stardom: Giannis Antetokounmpo, known as "The Greek Freak," was drafted by the Milwaukee Bucks in 2013. Over the subsequent years, he evolved from a promising young player into one of the league's premier superstars. By the 2020-2021 season, he had already won two MVP awards and been named to multiple All-NBA and All-Defensive Teams.

○ Previous Playoff Success: Antetokounmpo had led the Bucks to the Eastern Conference Finals in 2019 and was determined to win a championship with the team that had developed him from a rookie into a superstar.

2. The 2021 NBA Finals:

○ Teams and Matchup: The Milwaukee Bucks faced the Phoenix Suns in the Finals. The Suns, led by Chris Paul and Devin Booker, were making their first Finals appearance since 1993. The Bucks were seeking their first title since 1971.

○ Series Context: The series was tied 2-2 going into Game 6, with both teams showing exceptional skill and competitive spirit.

The Performance:
1. Game 6 Highlights:

○ Scoring Proficiency: Antetokounmpo's 50-point performance was characterized by his versatility and efficiency. He scored 15 field goals on 25 attempts and made 17 of 19 free throws. His ability to dominate both inside and outside the paint was evident throughout the game.

○ Key Contributions:

▪ First Half: Antetokounmpo scored 20 points in the first half, keeping the Bucks within striking distance of the Suns. His aggressive play on both ends of the floor was crucial in a tightly contested game.

▪ Second Half: He exploded for 30 points in the second half, including several clutch baskets. His performances in crucial moments helped the Bucks pull ahead and secure the win.

2. Defensive and Rebounding Impact:

○ Defense: Antetokounmpo's defensive contributions included several key blocks and rebounds. His presence in the paint was a significant factor in limiting the Suns' scoring opportunities.

○ Rebounding: He grabbed 14 rebounds, including critical offensive boards that extended possessions and led to additional scoring opportunities for the Bucks.

Impact and Significance:
1. Milwaukee Bucks:

○ Ending the Drought: The Bucks' victory in the 2021 NBA Finals ended a 50-year championship drought, bringing a long-awaited title to Milwaukee. Antetokounmpo's performance was pivotal in securing this historic win.

○ Franchise Legacy: The championship solidified the Bucks' place in NBA history and elevated their status as a top team in the league.

2. Antetokounmpo's Legacy:

○ Historic Achievement: Antetokounmpo's 50-point game in the Finals was one of the greatest performances in NBA Finals history. His dominant display of skill, athleticism, and mental toughness underscored his status as one of the league's elite players.

○ Impact on Career: The Finals MVP award was a career-defining accolade for Antetokounmpo, cementing his place as one of the greatest players of his generation and enhancing his legacy as a transformative force in the NBA.

3. NBA Impact:

○ Inspiration and Influence: Antetokounmpo's performance provided an inspirational example of excellence and perseverance. His ability to lead his team to victory through a dominant individual effort highlighted the impact that a superstar player can have on a team's success.

○ Market Impact: The Bucks' championship and Antetokounmpo's performance increased interest and excitement around the team, enhancing the global profile of the NBA and drawing attention to the city of Milwaukee.

Conclusion:

Giannis Antetokounmpo's 50-point game in Game 6 of the 2021 NBA Finals was a historic and defining moment in NBA history. His dominant performance not only secured the Milwaukee Bucks' first championship in half a century but also showcased his exceptional skill and leadership. Antetokounmpo's impact on the game and his contribution to the Bucks' victory cemented his legacy as one of the greatest players of his era and left an enduring mark on the sport of basketball.

Naomi Osaka's U.S. Open Victory (2020)

The Achievement:

Naomi Osaka's victory at the 2020 U.S. Open was not just a remarkable sporting achievement but also a powerful statement on social justice and resilience. Her win marked her second Grand Slam title and was notable for the way she used her platform to address racial issues and advocate for change.

Context and Background:

1. Osaka's Career Up to 2020:

○ Early Success: Naomi Osaka, born on October 16, 1997, in Chūō-ku, Osaka, Japan, had quickly risen through the ranks of tennis. She won her first Grand Slam title at the 2018 U.S. Open, defeating Serena Williams in a dramatic final.

○ Advocacy and Activism: Osaka had been increasingly vocal about social issues and racial justice. Her advocacy for these causes gained significant attention in the wake of the George Floyd protests and the broader Black Lives Matter movement.

2. The 2020 U.S. Open:

○ Tournament Context: The 2020 U.S. Open, held at the USTA Billie Jean King National Tennis Center in New York City, was impacted by the COVID-19 pandemic. The tournament took place with strict health protocols and without spectators.

○ Expectations: Osaka was a strong contender going into the tournament, known for her powerful game and previous Grand Slam success. Her performance in the lead-up to the tournament suggested she could be a major force.

The Performance:
1. Tournament Highlights:

○ Path to Victory: Osaka's path to the final was marked by dominant performances. She showcased her formidable skills with impressive wins against top players, including a standout victory over Serena Williams in the semi-finals.

○ Final Match: In the final, held on September 12, 2020, Osaka faced Victoria Azarenka. Osaka won in three sets, with a scoreline of 1-6, 6-3, 6-3. Her resilience and ability to recover from losing the first set were pivotal in securing the championship.

2. On-Court Excellence:

○ Power and Precision: Osaka's game was characterized by her powerful serves and aggressive groundstrokes. Her performance in the final demonstrated her ability to execute high-pressure shots and maintain composure in critical moments.

○ Mental Toughness: Osaka's mental resilience was evident as she overcame a challenging first set and adapted her strategy to secure victory.

Impact and Significance:
1. Social Justice Advocacy:

○ Protests and Symbolism: Throughout the tournament, Osaka used her platform to address racial injustice. She wore masks featuring the names of victims of police violence and racial injustice, including Breonna Taylor and George Floyd, during her matches.

○ Impact on Tennis: Osaka's advocacy highlighted the intersection of sports and social issues, drawing attention to the importance of athletes using their platforms to promote change. Her actions were widely praised and brought increased visibility to the Black Lives Matter movement.

2. Cultural Impact:

○ Inspiration and Influence: Osaka's victory and activism resonated with fans around the world. Her willingness to speak out on important social issues while achieving success on the court made her a powerful role model for young athletes and activists.

○ Global Recognition: Osaka's impact extended beyond tennis. Her efforts in advocating for social justice were recognized globally, and she was celebrated for her courage and commitment to making a difference.

3. Legacy and Future:

○ Career Milestone: The 2020 U.S. Open win solidified Osaka's status as one of the premier players in women's tennis. Her ability to combine exceptional athleticism with social advocacy set a new standard for athletes.

○ Ongoing Influence: Osaka's approach to using her platform for social change continues to influence athletes across various sports. Her legacy includes not only her achievements on the court but also her contributions to important societal conversations.

Conclusion:

Naomi Osaka's victory at the 2020 U.S. Open was a defining moment in tennis and sports history. Her triumph on the court was complemented by her powerful statement off the court, as she used her platform to address pressing social issues and advocate for justice. Osaka's combination of athletic excellence and activism highlighted the role of athletes in shaping cultural and social discourse, making her U.S. Open victory a landmark achievement with enduring significance.

<u>Kylian Mbappé's World Cup Brilliance (2018)</u>

The Achievement:

Kylian Mbappé's performance in the 2018 FIFA World Cup was a defining moment in football history. At just 19 years old, Mbappé emerged as a superstar, leading France to their second World Cup title with a series of electrifying performances that captivated fans worldwide.

Context and Background:

1. Mbappé's Career Up to 2018:

o Early Rise: Born on December 20, 1998, in Bondy, France, Kylian Mbappé demonstrated exceptional talent from a young age. By his teenage years, he had already become one of the most promising young players in European football.

o Professional Success: Mbappé's breakthrough came with AS Monaco, where he played a crucial role in the team's Ligue 1 title win in 2017. He soon joined Paris Saint-Germain (PSG), where he continued to impress with his speed, skill, and scoring ability.

2. The 2018 World Cup:

○ Tournament Overview: The 2018 FIFA World Cup was held in Russia from June 14 to July 15. France was one of the favorites, with a squad that combined young talent with experienced players.

○ Expectations: Mbappé entered the tournament as a highly anticipated young talent. His performances in the lead-up to the World Cup had generated significant excitement about his potential impact.

The Performance:
1. Tournament Highlights:

○ Group Stage: Mbappé showcased his abilities early in the tournament, scoring two goals in a 3-0 victory over Argentina in the Round of 16. His speed and skill were evident as he exploited Argentina's defense and scored a penalty.

○ Quarter-Final and Semi-Final: Mbappé's influence continued in the knockout stages. He played a key role in France's victories over Uruguay and Belgium, demonstrating his ability to perform under pressure.

○ Final Match: In the World Cup final against Croatia on July 15, 2018, Mbappé delivered a memorable performance. He scored a goal in the 65th minute, helping France secure a 4-2 victory and clinch the World Cup title. His goal made him the second teenager in history to score in a World Cup final, joining Pelé.

2. Performance Analysis:

○ Speed and Skill: Mbappé's extraordinary pace and dribbling ability were crucial to his success. His speed allowed him to outpace defenders and create scoring opportunities.

○ Composure and Precision: Despite his youth, Mbappé displayed remarkable composure and precision in front of goal. His ability to finish chances and make decisive plays was a testament to his exceptional talent.

Impact and Significance:
1. Global Recognition:

○ Stardom: Mbappé's performances at the World Cup catapulted him to international stardom. His combination of youth, talent, and success resonated with fans and experts alike, establishing him as one of the brightest stars in football.

○ Endorsements and Media: Following the World Cup, Mbappé became a global icon, attracting endorsements and media attention. His success on the world stage enhanced his profile and influence both on and off the field.

2. Impact on French Football:

○ National Pride: Mbappé's role in France's World Cup victory was a source of immense national pride. His performances helped France win their second World Cup, following their first in 1998.

○ Future of French Football: Mbappé's success signaled a promising future for French football. As a young talent with a significant impact, he was seen as a key figure in the next generation of French players.

3. Legacy and Future:

○ Career Milestone: Winning the World Cup at 19 was a historic achievement for Mbappé. It set a high bar for his future performances and solidified his place among football's elite players.

○ Influence on Young Players: Mbappé's success has inspired countless young players around the world. His story exemplifies how talent, hard work, and determination can lead to extraordinary achievements.

Conclusion:

Kylian Mbappé's brilliance in the 2018 World Cup was a landmark moment in football history. His electrifying performances and crucial goals helped France secure their second World Cup title and marked the emergence of a new football superstar. Mbappé's achievements at such a young age have left a lasting impact on the sport, setting the stage for an exciting future in football.

The Rise of E-Sports: A Look at the Growth and Impact of Competitive Gaming

Introduction: The rise of e-sports has transformed competitive gaming from a niche hobby into a global phenomenon. With millions of fans, professional players, and substantial financial investments, e-sports is now a major player in the sports and entertainment industries. This exploration into the growth and impact of competitive gaming reveals how e-sports has reshaped the landscape of both gaming and traditional sports.

1. The Origins of E-Sports:

- Early Beginnings:

  ○ 1970s-1980s: The concept of competitive gaming began with early arcade games and home consoles. The first video game competitions were held, such as the 1972 Stanford University Spacewar tournament, which is often cited as the first e-sports event.

  ○ 1990s: The rise of multiplayer games like "Quake" and "StarCraft" laid the groundwork for more organized competitive gaming. These games led to the formation of early e-sports leagues and tournaments.

- Formation of Competitive Leagues:

  ○ 2000s: The emergence of games like "Counter-Strike" and "Warcraft III" helped formalize competitive gaming. Organizations like Major League Gaming (MLG) were established, providing structured tournaments and leagues.

2. The Growth of E-Sports:
- Increased Popularity:

  ○ Streaming Platforms: The rise of platforms like Twitch and YouTube Gaming has made it easier for fans to follow e-sports events and players. Streaming has become a crucial part of e-sports culture, providing a direct connection between players and fans.

  ○ Mainstream Media: E-sports has gained recognition from traditional media outlets and sports networks, leading to increased coverage and legitimacy. Major networks like ESPN and TBS have aired e-sports events, further integrating e-sports into mainstream culture.

- Major Tournaments and Leagues:

o International Events: High-profile tournaments like "The International" (Dota 2), "League of Legends World Championship," and "CS

Major Championships" draw massive global audiences and feature substantial prize pools.

o Professional Leagues: Organizations such as the Overwatch League and the Call of Duty League have established professional e-sports leagues, featuring teams and players competing at the highest level.

3. The Impact of E-Sports:
- Economic Impact:

o Revenue and Sponsorships: E-sports generates significant revenue through sponsorships, advertising, and media rights. Major companies and brands invest heavily in e-sports, recognizing its growing influence and audience reach.

o Career Opportunities: E-sports has created numerous career opportunities, including professional players, coaches, analysts, content creators, and event organizers. The industry supports a diverse range of jobs and professions.

- Cultural Impact:

o Community and Culture: E-sports has cultivated a unique community and culture, with dedicated fans, team loyalty, and player followings. The culture surrounding e-sports often mirrors that of traditional sports, with fan clubs, merchandise, and fan events.

○ Diversity and Inclusion: E-sports has the potential to be more inclusive and diverse compared to traditional sports. It provides opportunities for players from various backgrounds and regions, contributing to a more global and inclusive gaming community.

4. Challenges and Future Directions:
● Challenges:

○ Regulation and Governance: As e-sports grows, issues related to regulation, governance, and fairness become increasingly important. Ensuring fair play and managing the integrity of competitions are ongoing challenges.

○ Health and Well-being: The health and well-being of players, including issues related to physical health, mental health, and work-life balance, are areas of concern. Organizations are increasingly focusing on providing support and resources for players.

● Future Directions:

○ Innovation and Technology: Advances in technology and gaming hardware will continue to shape the future of e-sports. Innovations in virtual reality, augmented reality, and gaming experiences are likely to influence the growth and evolution of competitive gaming.

○ Global Expansion: E-sports is expected to continue its global expansion, with increased participation and viewership in regions around the world. As the industry grows, it will likely see further integration with traditional sports and entertainment.

Conclusion: The rise of e-sports represents a significant shift in the landscape of competitive gaming and entertainment. From its early beginnings to its current status as a global phenomenon, e-sports has demonstrated its ability to captivate audiences, create economic opportunities, and shape cultural trends. As the industry continues to evolve, it will undoubtedly play a prominent role in the future of both gaming and sports.

Conclusion: The Legacy of Greatness

Reflecting on the Moments: How These Events Have Shaped Sports, Culture, and Society

The 50 greatest moments in sports history are more than just records, victories, or feats of athleticism; they are pivotal events that have shaped sports, influenced culture, and impacted society in profound ways. Here's a reflection on how these iconic moments have left their mark across various dimensions:

1. Shaping Sports:

1.1. Evolution of the Game:

- Innovation and Skill: Moments like Roger Bannister's sub-four-minute mile or Nadia Comăneci's perfect 10 revolutionized their respective sports by pushing the boundaries of what was considered possible. These achievements set new standards for skill and performance, inspiring future athletes to strive for similar heights.

- Strategy and Technique: The strategic brilliance of plays like Joe Montana's 92-yard Super Bowl drive or Bobby Thomson's "Shot Heard 'Round the World" demonstrated how individual brilliance can alter the course of a game, leading to changes in strategies and training approaches.

1.2. Dominance and Legacy:

- Unmatched Achievements: Records set by athletes like Michael Phelps, Wayne Gretzky, and Serena Williams not only defined their careers but also set benchmarks that future generations aspire to surpass. Their dominance in their sports has led to greater respect for their disciplines and a deeper appreciation for the level of excellence required to reach such heights.

2. Influencing Culture:

2.1. Cultural Icons and Heroes:

• Role Models: Athletes like Jackie Robinson, Muhammad Ali, and Billie Jean King became cultural icons through their performances and activism. Robinson's breaking of the color barrier, Ali's stand against the Vietnam War, and King's victory in the "Battle of the Sexes" transcended sports, influencing societal attitudes towards race, politics, and gender equality.

• Global Impact: Moments such as Usain Bolt's world record or Kylian Mbappé's World Cup brilliance captivated audiences worldwide, highlighting the global reach and unifying power of sports. These events brought people from diverse backgrounds together, celebrating shared human experiences and values.

2.2. Media and Popular Culture:

• Broadcasting and Fame: The rise of e-sports and iconic sports moments have been amplified through media and technology. The way these moments are covered and consumed has changed, with live broadcasts, social media, and digital platforms bringing sports into everyday life and expanding their influence.

3. Impacting Society:

3.1. Social Change and Movements:

• Activism and Awareness: The activism of athletes like Colin Kaepernick and the impact of moments like the 1968 Mexico City Olympics protest reflect how sports can be a powerful platform for social change. These events have sparked discussions and movements addressing issues such as racial inequality, human rights, and social justice.

• Inspiration and Aspiration: Achievements such as Simone Biles' Olympic dominance or Jim Abbott's no-hitter serve as powerful examples of overcoming adversity and achieving greatness. They inspire individuals to pursue their own dreams, regardless of challenges, and highlight the potential for sports to uplift and motivate people from all walks of life.

3.2. Economic and Commercial Impact:

• Economic Growth: The commercialization of sports, exemplified by the financial successes of events like the Super Bowl or the NBA Finals, has led to significant economic impacts. These moments drive revenue through sponsorships, media rights, and merchandise, contributing to the growth of the sports industry and creating economic opportunities for communities.

Conclusion:

The 50 greatest moments in sports history are more than just individual feats; they are reflective of broader societal trends and transformations. They shape the way we view sports, influence cultural norms, and impact social issues. Through their remarkable achievements, these moments have redefined sports, inspired generations, and left a lasting legacy on both the global stage and within our everyday lives. As we reflect on these events, it becomes clear that sports are not just games but a reflection of our collective aspirations, values, and humanity.

The Ever-Evolving World of Sports: The Potential for Future Iconic Moments and the Ongoing Impact of the Past

Sports are a dynamic and evolving realm, where past achievements continue to inspire and shape future events. As we look forward, the potential for new iconic moments is immense, driven by advances in technology, changes in societal values, and the relentless pursuit of excellence by athletes. At the same time, the impact of past moments remains profound, influencing the present and guiding future developments.

1. Potential for Future Iconic Moments:

1.1. Technological Advancements:

- Enhanced Training and Performance: The integration of advanced technologies such as virtual reality, AI-driven analytics, and biomechanical sensors is transforming how athletes train and compete. These innovations offer the potential for new records and unprecedented performances as athletes push the boundaries of human capability.

- Global Connectivity and Media: The rise of digital media and social platforms allows for instant global coverage and engagement. Future iconic moments could emerge from any corner of the world, as athletes leverage these platforms to reach new audiences and create viral phenomena.

1.2. Evolving Sports and New Disciplines:

- Emergence of New Sports: As new sports and activities gain popularity, they bring fresh opportunities for iconic moments. For instance, the growth of e-sports and adventure sports is creating new arenas for athletic achievement and memorable events.

- Adaptive Sports: The increasing visibility and development of adaptive sports for athletes with disabilities are leading to groundbreaking moments. These achievements highlight the resilience and skill of athletes overcoming significant challenges and expanding the definition of athletic excellence.

1.3. Societal and Cultural Shifts:

- Diversity and Inclusion: The ongoing focus on diversity and inclusion in sports is fostering a more inclusive environment where athletes from diverse backgrounds can achieve greatness. Future moments of significance may arise from this broader representation and the breaking of barriers related to gender, race, and ability.

- Social Activism: Athletes increasingly use their platforms to advocate for social and political causes. As this trend continues, future iconic moments may emerge from athletes' efforts to address pressing societal issues and inspire change.

2. Ongoing Impact of the Past:

2.1. Legacy and Inspiration:

- Setting Standards: Past iconic moments set new standards for excellence and performance. The records and achievements of athletes like Michael Phelps, Serena Williams, and Wayne Gretzky continue to serve as benchmarks and sources of inspiration for current and future athletes.

- Cultural Influence: Historical sports moments have shaped cultural narratives and societal values. For example, Jackie Robinson's breaking of the color barrier and Muhammad Ali's activism transcended sports, influencing broader social movements and shaping public discourse.

2.2. Evolving Traditions:

- Rituals and Ceremonies: The traditions and ceremonies associated with major sporting events, such as the Olympic Games and the Super Bowl, have evolved from historical precedents. These traditions are continuously refined and adapted to reflect contemporary values and practices.

- Historical Context: Understanding the historical context of past iconic moments helps frame current sports narratives and provides valuable lessons for athletes, coaches, and fans. The evolution of sports is deeply rooted in the events that have come before, influencing how sports are played, viewed, and celebrated.

2.3. Impact on Governance and Regulation:

- Rule Changes and Innovations: Iconic moments often lead to changes in rules and regulations. For example, technological advancements and controversies have led to new rules and review processes in various sports. These changes are influenced by past events and aim to enhance fairness, safety, and the integrity of the competition.

● Ethical Considerations: The ethical considerations surrounding sports, such as issues related to performance-enhancing drugs and athlete welfare, have evolved in response to past controversies and achievements. Ongoing debates and reforms are shaped by historical events and the lessons learned from them.

Conclusion:

The world of sports is a constantly evolving landscape where past achievements continue to influence and inspire future developments. As we look ahead, the potential for new iconic moments is vast, driven by technological advancements, evolving sports, and societal shifts. At the same time, the legacy of past moments remains a powerful force, shaping current practices, traditions, and values. The intersection of history and innovation ensures that sports will continue to produce remarkable achievements and moments of significance, reflecting our collective aspirations and the ever-changing nature of human endeavor.

Inspiration for the Future: Drawing Lessons from Iconic Sports Moments

The incredible stories of sports greatness that have defined our history offer more than just moments of triumph and celebration; they serve as powerful sources of inspiration for all aspects of life. Whether you're an athlete, a student, a professional, or simply someone navigating everyday challenges, the lessons embedded in these iconic moments can ignite your passion and drive you toward your own achievements. Here's how you can draw inspiration from these remarkable stories and apply it to your own journey:

1. Embrace the Spirit of Perseverance:

Overcoming Adversity: Moments like Jim Abbott's no-hitter or Kerri Strug's vault in the 1996 Olympics remind us of the power of perseverance. Despite facing significant challenges, these athletes achieved greatness through sheer determination and hard work. Apply this spirit to your own goals, understanding that setbacks and obstacles are part of the journey. Stay focused on your objectives, and let your perseverance guide you through difficulties.

Setting and Surpassing Goals: Tiger Woods' first Masters victory or Michael Phelps' record-breaking 8 gold medals illustrate the importance of setting ambitious goals and striving to surpass them. Set clear, measurable goals in your personal and professional life, and use the drive and dedication demonstrated by these athletes as motivation to push beyond your limits.

2. Embrace Innovation and Adaptation:

Pushing Boundaries: The groundbreaking performances of athletes like Roger Bannister or Secretariat highlight the importance of pushing boundaries and challenging the status quo. In your own pursuits, be open to innovation and new approaches. Embrace change and seek creative solutions to problems, just as these athletes have demonstrated through their extraordinary achievements.

Adapting to Change: As sports continue to evolve with advancements in technology and new disciplines, be adaptable in your own endeavors. Stay current with industry trends, embrace new skills, and remain flexible in the face of evolving challenges. This adaptability will help you stay relevant and successful in a constantly changing world.

3. Foster a Strong Work Ethic:

Dedication and Discipline: The success of athletes like Serena Williams and Wayne Gretzky is a testament to the power of a strong work ethic. Their achievements were built on countless hours of practice, dedication, and discipline. Cultivate a similar work ethic in your own life by committing to continuous improvement, focusing on your craft, and maintaining a disciplined approach to your goals.

Embracing Challenges: The resilience shown by athletes in overcoming obstacles serves as a reminder to embrace challenges rather than shy away from them. View challenges as opportunities for growth and development. By confronting difficulties head-on and maintaining a positive attitude, you can turn potential setbacks into valuable learning experiences.

4. Be a Catalyst for Positive Change:

Using Your Platform: The activism of athletes like Billie Jean King and Colin Kaepernick demonstrates the impact that individuals can have by using their platform to advocate for change. Identify issues that you are passionate about and find ways to contribute positively to your community or society. Your actions can inspire others and lead to meaningful change.

Inspiring Others: Just as past sports moments have inspired countless individuals, strive to be a source of inspiration for those around you. Share your journey, support others in their endeavors, and lead by example. Your achievements and positive attitude can motivate others to pursue their own dreams and overcome their own challenges.

5. Celebrate and Reflect on Achievements:

Acknowledging Success: The celebration of historic moments in sports underscores the importance of acknowledging and celebrating achievements, both big and small. Take time to recognize your own successes and milestones, and celebrate your progress. This not only boosts your confidence but also provides motivation to continue striving for excellence.

Learning from the Past: Reflect on the lessons and inspiration from past sports moments. Use these insights to guide your own path, understand the values of resilience, innovation, and dedication, and apply them to your personal and professional endeavors. The stories of greatness serve as powerful reminders of what is possible when we commit to our goals and pursue them with passion.

Conclusion:

The iconic moments in sports history are more than just records and victories; they are beacons of inspiration that transcend the realm of athletics. By embracing the perseverance, innovation, work ethic, and positive change exemplified by these moments, you can find motivation for your own journey. Let the stories of past greatness fuel your ambition, guide your actions, and inspire you to achieve your own milestones. In doing so, you contribute to a legacy of excellence and become part of a continuing narrative of success and inspiration.

www.ingramcontent.com/pod-product-compliance
Lightning Source LLC
Chambersburg PA
CBHW051234130726
47988CB00001B/346